MOLIÈRE'S
THE LEARNED
LADIES

IN A NEW ENGLISH VERSE TRANSLATION

BY RICHARD WILBUR

★

★

DRAMATISTS
PLAY SERVICE
INC.

CHARACTERS

CHRYSALE, a well-to-do bourgeois.

PHILAMINTE, Chrysale's wife.

ARMANDE and HENRIETTE,
  daughters of Chrysale and Philaminte.

ARISTE, Chrysale's brother.

BÉLISE, Chrysale's sister.

CLITANDRE, Henriette's suitor.

TRISSOTIN, a wit.

VADIUS, a scholar.

MARTINE, kitchen-maid.

LÉPINE, a servant.

JULIEN, valet to Vadius.

A NOTARY.

THE SCENE: Chrysale's house in Paris.

For

GILBERT PARKER

The Learned Ladies

ACT ONE

SCENE 1

Armande, Henriette

ARMANDE.
What, Sister! Are you truly of a mind
To leave your precious maidenhood behind,
And give yourself in marriage to a man?
Can you be harboring such a vulgar plan?
HENRIETTE.
Yes, Sister.
ARMANDE.
   Yes, you say! When have I heard
So odious and sickening a word?
HENRIETTE.
Why does the thought of marriage so repel you?
ARMANDE.
Fie, fie! For shame!
HENRIETTE.
    But what—
ARMANDE.
       For shame, I tell you!
Can you deny what sordid scenes are brought
To the mind's eye by that distasteful thought,
What coarse, degrading images arise,
What shocking things it makes one visualize?
Do you not shudder, Sister, and grow pale
At what this thought you're thinking would entail?
HENRIETTE.
It would entail, as I conceive it, one
Husband, some children, and a house to run;
In all of which, it may as well be said,
I find no cause for loathing or for dread.

5

ARMANDE.
Alas! Such bondage truly appeals to you?
HENRIETTE.
At my young age, what better could I do
Than join myself in wedded harmony
To one I love, and who in turn loves me,
And through the deepening bond of man and wife
Enjoy a blameless and contented life?
Does such a union offer no attractions?
ARMANDE.
Oh dear, you crave such squalid satisfactions!
How can you choose to play a petty role,
Dull and domestic, and content your soul
With joys no loftier than keeping house
And raising brats, and pampering a spouse?
Let common natures, vulgarly inclined,
Concern themselves with trifles of that kind.
Aspire to nobler objects, seek to attain
To keener joys upon a higher plane,
And, scorning gross material things as naught,
Devote yourself, as we have done, to thought.
We have a mother to whom all pay honor
For erudition; model yourself upon her;
Yes, prove yourself her daughter, as I have done,
Join in the quest for truth that she's begun,
And learn how love of study can impart
A sweet enlargement to the mind and heart.
Why marry, and be the slave of him you wed?
Be married to philosophy instead,
Which lifts us up above mankind, and gives
All power to reason's pure imperatives,
Thus rendering our bestial natures tame
And mastering those lusts which lead to shame.
A love of reason, a passion for the truth,
Should quite suffice one's heart in age or youth,
And I am moved to pity when I note
On what low objects certain women dote.
HENRIETTE.
But Heaven, in its wise omnipotence,
Endows us all with differing gifts and bents,

And all souls are not fashioned, I'm afraid,
Of the stuff of which philosophers are made.
If yours was born for soaring to the heights
Of learning, and for speculative flights,
My own weak spirit, Sister, has from birth
Clung to the homelier pleasures of the earth.
Let's not oppose what Heaven has decreed,
But simply follow where our instincts lead.
You, through the towering genius you possess,
Shall dwell in philosophic loftiness,
While my prosaic nature, here below,
Shall taste such joys as marriage can bestow.
Thus, though our lives contrast with one another,
We each shall emulate our worthy mother—
You, in your quest for rational excellence,
I, in the less refined delights of sense;
You, in conceptions lofty and ethereal,
I in conceptions rather more material.
ARMANDE.
Sister, the person whom one emulates
Ought to be followed for her finer traits.
If someone's worthy to be copied, it's
Not for the way in which she coughs and spits.
HENRIETTE.
You and your intellect would not be here
If Mother's traits had all been fine, my dear,
And it's most fortunate for you that she
Was not wed solely to philosophy.
Relent, and tolerate in me, I pray,
That urge through which you saw the light of day,
And do not bid me be like you, and scorn
The hopes of some small scholar to be born.
ARMANDE.
Your mind, I see, is stupidly contrary,
And won't give up its stubborn wish to marry.
But tell me, do, of this intended match:
Surely it's not Clitandre you aim to catch?
HENRIETTE.
Why not? Of what defects could one accuse him?
Would I be vulgar if I were to choose him?

7

ARMANDE.
No. But I don't think much of your design
To lure away a devotee of mine;
Clitandre, as the world well knows, has sighed
And yearned for me, and sought me as his bride.
HENRIETTE.
Yes; but such sighs, arising as they do
From base affections, are as naught to you;
Marriage is something you have risen above,
And fair philosophy has all your love.
Since, then, Clitandre isn't necessary
To your well-being, may he and I not marry?
ARMANDE.
Though reason bids us shun the baits of sense,
We still may take delight in compliments;
We may refuse a man, yet be desirous
That still he pay us homage, and admire us.
HENRIETTE.
I never sought to make him discontinue
His worship of the noble soul that's in you;
But once you had refused him, I felt free
To take the love which he then offered me.
ARMANDE.
When a rejected suitor, full of spite,
Claims to adore you, can you trust him quite?
Do you really think he loves you? Are you persuaded
That his intense desire for me has faded?
HENRIETTE.
Yes, Sister, I believe it; he's told me so.
ARMANDE.
Sister, you're gullible; as you should know,
His talk of leaving me and loving you
Is self-deceptive bluster, and quite untrue.
HENRIETTE.
Perhaps; however, Sister, if you'd care
To learn with me the facts of this affair,
I see Clitandre coming; I'm sure, my dear,
That if we ask, he'll make his feelings clear.

SCENE 2

Clitandre, Armande, Henriette

HENRIETTE.
My sister has me in uncertainties
As to your heart's affections. If you please,
Clitandre, tell us where your feelings lie,
And which of us may claim you—she, or I.
ARMANDE.
No, I'll not join in making you reveal
So publicly the passion which you feel;
You are, I'm sure, reluctant to confess
Your private feelings under such duress.
CLITANDRE. (*To Armande.*)
Madam, my heart, unused to sly pretense,
Does not reluct to state its sentiments;
I'm not at all embarrassed, and can proclaim
Wholeheartedly, without reserve or shame,
That she whom I most honor, hold most dear,
And whose devoted slave I am . . . ·
                (*Gesturing toward Henriette.*)
                                        is here.
Take no offense; you've nothing to resent:
You've made your choice, and so should be content.
Your charms enthralled me once, as many a sigh
And warm profession served to testify;
I offered you a love which could not fade,
Yet you disdained the conquest you had made.
Beneath your tyrant gaze, my soul has borne
A hundred bitter slights, and every scorn,
Till, wearying at last of whip and chain
It hungered for a bondage more humane.
Such have I found, *Madame,* in these fair eyes,
                (*Gesturing once more toward Henriette.*)
Whose kindness I shall ever love and prize:
They have not spurned the man you cast aside,
And, warmed by their regard, my tears have dried.
Now nothing could persuade me to be free
Of this most amiable captivity,

9

And I entreat you, Madam, do not strive
To cause my former feelings to revive,
Or sway my heart as once you did, for I
Propose to love this lady till I die.

ARMANDE.

Well, Sir! What makes you fancy that one might
Regard you with a jealous appetite?
You're fatuous indeed to harbor such
A thought, and very brash to say as much.

HENRIETTE.

Steady now, Sister. Where's that discipline
Of soul which reins one's lower nature in,
And keeps one's temper under firm command?

ARMANDE.

And you, dear: are your passions well in hand
When you propose to wed a man without
The leave of those who brought your life about?
You owe your parents a complete submission,
And may not love except by their permission;
Your heart is theirs, and you may not bestow it;
To do so would be wicked, and you know it.

HENRIETTE.

I'm very grateful to be thus instructed
In how these matters ought to be conducted.
And just to prove to you that I've imbibed
Your teachings, I shall do as you've prescribed:
Clitandre, I should thank you if you went
And gained from my dear parents their consent,
So that, without the risk of wickedness,
I could return the love which you profess.

CLITANDRE.

Now that I have your gracious leave, I'll bend
My every effort towards that happy end.

ARMANDE.

You look triumphant, Sister, and appear
To think me vexed by what has happened here.

HENRIETTE.

By no means, Sister. I well know how you've checked
Your senses with the reins of intellect,
And how no foolish weakness could disturb

10

A heart so disciplined by wisdom's curb.
I'm far from thinking you upset; indeed,
I know you'll give me the support I need,
Help win my parents to Clitandre's side,
And speed the day when I may be his bride.
Do lend your influence, Sister, to promote—
ARMANDE.
What childish teasing, Sister! And how you gloat
At having made a cast-off heart your prize!
HENRIETTE.
Cast-off or not, it's one you don't despise.
Had you the chance to get it back from me,
You'd gladly pick it up on bended knee.
ARMANDE.
I shall not stoop to answer that. I deem
This whole discussion silly in the extreme.
HENRIETTE.
It is indeed, and you do well to end it.
Your self-control is great, and I commend it.

SCENE 3

Clitandre, Henriette

HENRIETTE.
Your frank avowal left her quite unnerved.
CLITANDRE.
Such frankness was no less than she deserved;
Given her haughty airs and foolish pride,
My blunt words were entirely justified.
But now, since you have given me leave, I'll seek
Your father—
HENRIETTE.
         It's to Mother you should speak.
My gentle father would say yes, of course,
But his decrees, alas, have little force;
Heaven blessed him with a mild, concessive soul
Which yields in all things to his wife's control.
It's she who rules the house, requiring him

11

To treat as law her every royal whim.
I wish that you were more disposed to please
My mother, and indulge my Aunt Bélise,
By humoring their fancies, and thereby
Making them view you with a kindly eye.
CLITANDRE.
My heart's too frank for that; I could not praise,
Even in your sister, such outlandish ways,
And female sages aren't my cup of tea.
A woman should know something, I agree,
Of every subject, but this proud desire
To pose as erudite I can't admire.
I like a woman who, though she may know
The answers, does not always let it show;
Who keeps her studies secret and, in fine,
Though she's enlightened, feels no need to shine
By means of pompous word and rare quotation
And brilliance on the slightest provocation.
I much respect your mother; nonetheless,
I can't encourage her in foolishness,
Agree with everything she says, and laud
Her intellectual hero—who's a fraud.
I loathe her Monsieur Trissotin; how can
She so esteem so ludicrous a man,
And class with men of genius and of vision
A dunce whose works meet always with derision,
A bore whose dreadful books end, one and all,
As wrapping-paper in some market-stall?
HENRIETTE.
All that he writes or speaks I find a bore;
I could agree with all you say, and more;
But since the creature has my mother's ear,
He's someone you should cultivate, I fear.
A lover seeks the good opinion of
All who surround the object of his love,
And, so that no one will oppose his passion,
Treats even the house-dog in a courtly fashion.
CLITANDRE.
You're right; yet Trissotin, I must admit
So irks me that there's no controlling it.
I can't, to gain his advocacy, stoop

12

To praise the works of such a nincompoop.
It was those works which introduced me to him;
Before I ever saw the man, I knew him;
From the vile way he wrote, I saw with ease
What, in the flesh, must be his qualities:
The absolute presumption, the complete
And dauntless nature of his self-conceit,
The calm assurance of superior worth
Which renders him the smuggest man on earth,
So that he stands in awe and hugs himself
Before his volumes ranged upon the shelf,
And would not trade his baseless reputation
For that of any general in the nation.
HENRIETTE.
If you could see all that, you've got good eyes.
CLITANDRE.
I saw still more; for I could visualize,
By studying his dreadful poetry,
Just what the poet's lineaments must be;
I pictured him so truly that, one day,
Seeing a foppish man in the *Palais,*
I said, "That's Trissotin, by God!"—and found,
Upon enquiry, that my hunch was sound.
HENRIETTE.
What a wild story!
CLITANDRE.

            Not at all; it's true.
But here's your aunt. If you'll permit me to,
I'll tell her of our hopes, in hopes that she
Will urge your mother to approve of me.

SCENE 4

Clitandre, Bélise

CLITANDRE.
Madam, permit a lover's heart to seize
This happy opportunity, if you please,
To tell you of his passion, and reveal—

BÉLISE.
Hold, Sir! Don't say too baldly what you feel.
If you belong, Sir, to the ranks of those
Who love me, let your eyes alone disclose
Your sentiments, and do not tell me bluntly
Of coarse desires which only could affront me.
Adore me if you will, but do not show it
In such a way that I'll be forced to know it;
Worship me inwardly, and I shall brook it
If, through your silence, I can overlook it;
But should you dare to speak of it outright,
I'll banish you forever from my sight.
CLITANDRE.
My passions, Madam, need cause you no alarms;
It's Henriette who's won me by her charms,
And I entreat your generous soul to aid me
In my design to wed that charming lady.
BÉLISE.
Ah, what a subtle dodge; you should be proud;
You're very artful, it must be allowed;
In all the novels that I've read, I've never
Encountered any subterfuge so clever.
CLITANDRE.
Madam, I meant no witty indirection;
I've spoken truly of my heart's affection.
By Heaven's will, by ties that cannot part,
I'm bound to Henriette with all my heart;
It's Henriette I cherish, as I've said,
And Henriette whom I aspire to wed.
All that I ask of you is that you lend
Your influence to help me gain that end.
BÉLISE.
I well divine the hopes which you have stated,
And how the name you've used should be translated.
A clever substitution, Sir; and I
Shall use the selfsame code in my reply:
"Henriette" disdains to wed, and those who burn
For her must hope for nothing in return.
CLITANDRE.
Madam, why make things difficult? Why insist
Upon supposing what does not exist?

BÉLISE.
Good heavens, Sir, don't stand on ceremony,
Denying what your looks have often shown me.
Let it suffice, Sir, that I am contented
With this oblique approach you have invented,
And that, beneath such decorous disguise,
Your homage is acceptable in my eyes,
Provided that you make no overture
Which is not noble, rarefied, and pure.
CLITANDRE.
But—
BÉLISE.
      Hush. Farewell. It's time our talk was ended.
I've said, already, more than I intended.
CLITANDRE.
You're quite mistaken—
BÉLISE.
                I'm blushing, can't you see?
All this has overtaxed my modesty.
CLITANDRE.
I'm hanged if I love you, Madam! This is absurd.
BÉLISE.
No, no, I mustn't hear another word.
          (She exits.)
CLITANDRE.
The devil take her and her addled brain!
What stubborn fancies she can entertain!
Well, I'll turn elsewhere, and shall hope to find
Support from someone with a balanced mind.

ACT TWO

Scene 1

Ariste

ARISTE. (*To Clitandre, who is making his exit.*)
Yes, yes, I'll urge and plead as best I can, Sir,
Then hasten back to you and bring his answer.
Lovers! How very much they have to say,
And what extreme impatience they display!
Never—

Scene 2

Chrysale, Ariste

ARISTE.
   Ah! God be with you, Brother dear.
CHRYSALE.
And you, dear Brother.
ARISTE.
     D'you know what brings me here?
CHRYSALE.
No, but I'll gladly learn of it; do tell.
ARISTE.
I think you know Clitandre rather well?
CHRYSALE.
Indeed; he calls here almost every day.
ARISTE.
And what is your opinion of him, pray?
CHRYSALE.
He's a man of honor, breeding, wit, and spirit;
I know few lads of comparable merit.
ARISTE.
Well, I am here at his request; I'm glad
To learn that you think highly of the lad.

CHRYSALE.
I knew his father well, during my stay
In Rome.
ARISTE.

       Ah, good.
CHRYSALE.

            A fine man.
ARISTE.

                   So they say.
CHRYSALE.
We were both young then, twenty-eight or so,
And a pair of dashing gallants, I'll have you know.
ARISTE.
I'm sure of it.
CHRYSALE.

           Oh, those dark-eyed Roman maids!
The whole town talked about our escapades,
And weren't the husbands jealous!
ARISTE.

                  Ho! No doubt!
But let me broach the matter I came about.

SCENE 3

Bélise, entering quietly and listening, Chrysale, Ariste

ARISTE.
I'm here to speak for young Clitandre, and let
You know of his deep love for Henriette.
CHRYSALE.
He loves my daughter?
ARISTE.

            Yes. Upon my honor,
I've never seen such passion; he dotes upon her.
BÉLISE. (*To Ariste.*)
No, no; I see what's happened. You're unaware
Of the true character of this affair.
ARISTE.
What, Sister?

BÉLISE.

   Clitandre has misled you, Brother:
The passion which he feels is for another.
ARISTE.
Oh, come. He doesn't love Henriette? Then how—
BÉLISE.
I'm certain of it.
ARISTE.

   He said he did, just now.
BÉLISE.
Of course.
ARISTE.

   He sent me here, please understand,
To ask her father for the lady's hand.
BÉLISE.
Splendid.
ARISTE.

   What's more, his ardor is so great
That I'm to urge an early wedding-date.
BÉLISE.
Oh, how delightful; what obliquity!
We use the name of "Henriette," you see,
As a code-word and camouflage concealing
The actual object of his tender feeling.
But I'll consent, now, to enlighten you.
ARISTE.
Well, Sister, since you know so much, please do
Tell us with whom his true affections lie.
BÉLISE.
You wish to know?
ARISTE.

   I do.
BÉLISE.

   It's I.
ARISTE.

   You?
BÉLISE.

   I.
ARISTE.
Well, Sister!

BÉLISE.

        What do you mean by *well*? My word,
Why should you look surprised at what you've heard?
My charms are evident, in my frank opinion,
And more than one heart's under their dominion.
Dorante, Damis, Cléonte, Valère—all these
Are proof of my attractive qualities.

ARISTE.

These men all love you?

BÉLISE.

                Yes, with all their might.

ARISTE.

They've said so?

BÉLISE.

            None has been so impolite:
They've worshipped me as one from heaven above,
And not presumed to breathe a word of love.
Mute signs, however, have managed to impart
The keen devotion of each humble heart.

ARISTE.

Damis is almost never seen here. Why?

BÉLISE.

His reverence for me has made him shy.

ARISTE.

Dorante reviles you in the harshest fashion.

BÉLISE.

He's seized, at times, by fits of jealous passion.

ARISTE.

Cléonte has lately married; so has Valère.

BÉLISE.

That was because I drove them to despair.

ARISTE.

Sister, you're prone to fantasies, I fear.

CHRYSALE. (*To Bélise.*)

Get rid of these chimeras, Sister dear.

BÉLISE.

Chimeras! Well! Chimeras, did you say?
I have chimeras! Well, how very gay!
May all your thoughts, dear Brothers, be as clear as
Those which you dared, just now, to call *chimeras!*

19

SCENE 4

Chrysale, Ariste

CHRYSALE.
Our sister's mad.
ARISTE.
                    And growing madder daily.
But, once more, let's discuss our business, may we?
Clitandre longs to marry Henriette,
And asks your blessing. What answer shall he get?
CHRYSALE.
No need to ask. I readily agree.
His wish does honor to my family.
ARISTE.
He has, as you well know, no great amount
Of worldly goods—
CHRYSALE.
                    Ah, gold's of no account:
He's rich in virtue, that most precious ore;
His father and I were bosom friends, what's more.
ARISTE.
Let's go make certain that your wife concurs.
CHRYSALE.
I've given my consent; no need for hers.
ARISTE.
True, Brother; still, 't'would do no harm if your
Decision had her strong support, I'm sure.
Let's both go—
CHRYSALE.
                    Nonsense, that's a needless move;
I'll answer for my wife. She will approve.
ARISTE.
But—
CHRYSALE.
        No. Enough. I'll deal with her. Don't worry.
The business will be settled in a hurry.
ARISTE.
So be it. I'll go consult with Henriette,
And then—

CHRYSALE.
The thing's as good as done; don't fret.
I'll tell my wife about it, without delay.

SCENE 5

Martine, Chrysale

MARTINE.
Ain't that my luck! It's right, what people say—
When you hang a dog, first give him a bad name.
Domestic service! It's a losing game.
CHRYSALE.
Well, well, Martine! What's up?
MARTINE.
You want to know?
CHRYSALE.
Why, yes.
MARTINE.
What's up is, Madam's let me go.
CHRYSALE.
She's let you go?
MARTINE.
Yes, given me the sack.
CHRYSALE.
But why? Whatever for?
MARTINE.
She says she'll whack
Me black and blue if I don't clear out of here.
CHRYSALE.
No, you shall stay; you've served me well, my dear.
My wife's a bit short-tempered at times, and fussy:
But this won't do. I'll—

SCENE 6

Philaminte, Bélise, Chrysale, Martine

PHILAMINTE. (Seeing Martine.)
What! Still here, you hussy!

Be off, you trollop; leave my house this minute,
And mind you never again set foot within it!
CHRYSALE.
Gently, now.
PHILAMINTE.
        No, it's settled.
CHRYSALE.
                But—
PHILAMINTE.
                      Off with her!
CHRYSALE.
What crime has she committed, to incur—
PHILAMINTE.
So! You defend the girl!
CHRYSALE.
                No, that's not so.
PHILAMINTE.
Are you taking her side against me?
CHRYSALE.
                      Heavens, no;
I merely asked the nature of her offense.
PHILAMINTE.
Would I, without good reason, send her hence?
CHRYSALE.
Of course not; but employers should be just—
PHILAMINTE.
Enough! I bade her leave, and leave she must.
CHRYSALE.
Quite so, quite so. Has anyone denied it?
PHILAMINTE.
I won't be contradicted. I can't abide it.
CHRYSALE.
Agreed.
PHILAMINTE.
       If you were a proper husband, you
Would take my side, and share my outrage, too.
CHRYSALE.
I do, dear.
          (*Turning towards Martine.*)
        Wench! My wife is right to rid
This house of one who's done the thing you did.

MARTINE.
What did I do?
CHRYSALE. (*Aside.*)
                        Alas, you have me there.
PHILAMINTE.
She takes a light view, still, of this affair.
CHRYSALE.
What caused your anger? How did all this begin?
Did she break some mirror, or piece of porcelain?
PHILAMINTE.
Do you suppose that I'd be angry at her,
And bid her leave, for such a trifling matter?
CHRYSALE. (*To Martine.*)
What can this mean? (*To Philaminte.*) Is the crime, then,
                                    very great?
PHILAMINTE.
Of course it is. Would I exaggerate?
CHRYSALE.
Did she, perhaps, by inadvertence, let
Some vase be stolen, or some china-set?
PHILAMINTE.
That would be nothing.
CHRYSALE. (*To Martine.*)
                        Blast, girl, what can this be?
                    (*To Philaminte.*)
Have you caught the chit in some dishonesty?
PHILAMINTE.
Far worse than that.
CHRYSALE.
                    Far worse than that?
PHILAMINTE.
                                            Far worse.
CHRYSALE. (*To Martine.*)
For shame, you strumpet! (*To Philaminte.*) Has she been so
                                                perverse—
PHILAMINTE.
This creature, who for insolence has no peer,
Has, after thirty lessons, shocked my ear
By uttering a low, plebeian word
Which Vaugelas deems unworthy to be heard.

CHRYSALE.
Is *that*—?
PHILAMINTE.

And she persists in her defiance
Of that which is the basis of all science—
Grammar! which even the mightiest must obey,
And whose pure laws hold princes in their sway.
CHRYSALE.
I was sure she'd done the worst thing under the sun.
PHILAMINTE.
What! You don't find it monstrous, what she's done?
CHRYSALE.
Oh, yes.
PHILAMINTE.

I'd love to hear you plead her case!
CHRYSALE.
Not I!
BÉLISE.

It's true, her speech is a disgrace.
How long we've taught her language and its laws!
Yet still she butchers every phrase or clause.
MARTINE.
I'm sure your preachings is all well and good,
But I wouldn't talk your jargon if I could.
PHILAMINTE.
She dares describe as jargon a speech that's based
On reason, and good usage, and good taste!
MARTINE.
If people get the point, that's speech to me;
Fine words don't have no use that I can see.
PHILAMINTE.
Hark! There's a sample of her style again!
"Don't have no!"
BÉLISE.

O ineducable brain!
How futile have our efforts been to teach
Your stubborn mind the rules of proper speech!
You've coupled *don't* with *no*. I can't forgive
That pleonasm, that double negative.

MARTINE.
Good Lord, Ma'am, I ain't studious like you;
I just talk plain, the way my people do.
PHILAMINTE.
What ghastly solecisms!
BÉLISE.

                         I could faint!

PHILAMINTE.
How the ear shudders at the sound of "ain't!"
BÉLISE. (*To Martine*.)
With ignorance like yours, one struggles vainly.
"Plain" is an adjective; the adverb's "plainly."
Shall grammar be abused by you forever?
MARTINE.
Me abuse Gram'ma? Or Gram'pa either? Never!
PHILAMINTE.
Dear God!
BÉLISE.

               What I said was "grammar." You misheard.
I've told you about the origin of the word.
MARTINE.
Let it come from Passy, Pontoise, or Chaillot;
It's Greek to me.
BÉLISE.

               Alas, what *do* you know,
You peasant? It is grammar which lays down
The laws which govern adjective and noun,
And verb, and subject.
MARTINE.

               Madam, I'd just be lying
If I said I knew those people.
PHILAMINTE.

               Oh, how trying!
BÉLISE.
Girl, those are parts of speech, and we must be
At pains to make those parts of speech agree.
MARTINE.
Let them agree or squabble, what does it matter?

25

PHILAMINTE. (*To her sister-in-law.*)
Ah, mercy, let's be done with all this chatter!
(*To her husband.*)
Sir! Will you bid her go and leave me in peace?
CHRYSALE.
Yes, yes. (*Aside.*) I must give in to her caprice.
(*To Martine.*)
Martine, don't vex her further; you'd best depart.
PHILAMINTE.
So, you're afraid to wound her little heart!
The hussy! Must you be so sweet and mild?
CHRYSALE.
Of course not. (*Loudly.*) Wench, be off!
(*Softly, to Martine.*)
Go, go, poor child.

SCENE 7

Philaminte, Chrysale, Bélise

CHRYSALE.
Well, you have had your way, and she is gone;
But I don't think much of the way you've carried on.
The girl is good at what she does, and you've
Dismissed her for a trifle. I don't approve.
PHILAMINTE.
Would you have me keep her in my service here
To give incessant anguish to my ear
By constant barbarisms, and the breach
Of every law of reason and good speech,
Patching the mangled discourse which she utters
With coarse expressions from the city's gutters?
BÉLISE.
It's true, her talk can drive one out of one's wits.
Each day, she tears dear Vaugelas to bits,
And the least failings of this pet of yours
Are vile cacophonies and non-sequiturs.
CHRYSALE.
Who cares if she offends some grammar-book,

So long as she doesn't offend us as a cook?
If she makes a tasty salad, it seems to me
Her subjects and her verbs need not agree.
Let all her talk be barbarous, if she'll not
Burn up my beef or over-salt the pot.
It's food, not language, that I'm nourished by.
Vaugelas can't teach you how to bake a pie;
Malherbe, Balzac, for all their learnèd rules,
Might, in a kitchen, have been utter fools.
PHILAMINTE.
I'm stunned by what you've said, and shocked at seeing
How you, who claim the rank of human being,
Rather than rise on spiritual wings,
Give all your care to base, material things.
This rag, the body—does it matter so?
Should its desires detain us here below?
Should we not soar aloft, and scorn to heed it?
CHRYSALE.
My body is myself, and I aim to feed it.
It's a rag, perhaps, but one of which I'm fond.
BÉLISE.
Brother, 'twixt flesh and spirit there's a bond;
Yet, as the best minds of the age have stated,
The claims of flesh must be subordinated,
And it must be our chief delight and care
To feast the soul on philosophic fare.
CHRYSALE.
I don't know what your soul's been eating of late,
But it's not a balanced diet, at any rate;
You show no womanly solicitude
For—
PHILAMINTE.
              "Womanly!" That word is old and crude.
It reeks, in fact, of its antiquity.
BÉLISE.
It sounds old-fashioned and absurd to me.
CHRYSALE.
See here; I can't contain myself; I mean
To drop the mask for once, and vent my spleen.
The whole world thinks you mad, and I am through—

PHILAMINTE.
How's that, Sir?
CHRYSALE. (*To Bélise.*)

            Sister, I am addressing *you.*
The least mistake in speech you can't forgive,
But how mistakenly you choose to live!
I'm sick of those eternal books you've got;
In my opinion, you should burn the lot,
Save for that Plutarch where I press my collars,
And leave the studious life to clerks and scholars;
And do throw out, if I may be emphatic,
That great long frightful spyglass in the attic,
And all these other gadgets, and do it soon.
Stop trying to see what's happening in the moon.
And look what's happening in your household here,
Where everything is upside-down and queer.
For a hundred reasons, it's neither meet nor right
That a woman study and be erudite.
To teach her children manners, overlook
The household, train the servants and the cook,
And keep a thrifty budget—these should be
Her only study and philosophy.
Our fathers had a saying which made good sense:
A woman's polished her intelligence
Enough, they said, if she can pass the test
Of telling a pair of breeches from a vest.
Their wives read nothing, yet their lives were good;
Domestic lore was all they understood,
And all their books were needle and thread, with which
They made their daughters' trousseaus, stitch by stitch.
But women scorn such modest arts of late;
They want to scribble and to cogitate;
No mystery is too deep for them to plumb.
Is there a stranger house in Christendom
Than mine, where women are as mad as hatters,
And everything is known except what matters?
They know how Mars, the moon, and Venus turn,
And Saturn too, that's none of my concern,
And what with all this vain and far-fetched learning,
They don't know if my roast of beef is burning.

My servants, who now aspire to culture too,
Do anything but what they're paid to do;
Thinking is all this household thinks about,
And reasoning has driven reason out.
One spoils a sauce, while reading the dictionary;
One mumbles verses when I ask for sherry;
Because they ape the follies they've observed
In you, I keep six servants and am not served.
Just one poor wench remained who hadn't caught
The prevalent disease of lofty thought,
And now, since Vaugelas might find her lacking
In grammar, you've blown up and sent her packing.
Sister (I'm speaking to you, as I said before,)
These goings-on I censure and deplore.
I'm tired of visits from these pedants versed
In Latin, and that ass Trissotin's the worst.
He's flattered you in many a wretched sonnet;
There's a great swarm of queer bees in his bonnet;
Each time he speaks, one wonders what he's said;
I think, myself, that he's crazy in the head.
PHILAMINTE.
Dear God, what brutishness of speech and mind!
BÉLISE.
Could particles more grossly be combined,
Or atoms form an aggregate more crass?
And can we be of the same blood? Alas,
I hate myself because we two are kin,
And leave this scene in horror and chagrin.

SCENE 8

Philaminte, Chrysale

PHILAMINTE.
Have you other shots to fire, or are you through?
CHRYSALE.
I? No, no. No more quarrelling. That will do.
Let's talk of something else. As we've heard her state,
Your eldest daughter scorns to take a mate.

29

She's a philosopher—mind you, I'm not complaining;
She's had the finest of maternal training.
But her younger sister's otherwise inclined,
And I've a notion that it's time to find
A match for Henriette—

PHILAMINTE.

                             Exactly, and
I'll now inform you of the match I've planned.
That Trissotin whose visits you begrudge,
And whom you so contemptuously judge,
Is, I've decided, the appropriate man.
If you can't recognize his worth, I can.
Let's not discuss it; it's quite unnecessary;
I've thought things through; it's he whom she should marry.
Don't tell her of my choice, however; I choose
To be the first to let her know the news.
That she will listen to reason I have no doubt,
And if you seek to meddle, I'll soon find out.

SCENE 9

Ariste, Chrysale

ARISTE.
Ah, Brother; your wife's just leaving, and it's clear
That you and she have had a conference here.

CHRYSALE.
Yes.

ARISTE.
     Well, shall Clitandre have his Henriette?
Is your wife willing? Can the date be set?

CHRYSALE.
Not altogether.

ARISTE.
                 What, she refuses?

CHRYSALE.
                          No.

ARISTE.
Is she wavering, then?

30

CHRYSALE.

I wouldn't describe her so.

ARISTE.

What, then?

CHRYSALE.

There's someone else whom she prefers.

ARISTE.

For a son-in-law?

CHRYSALE.

Yes.

ARISTE.

Who is this choice of hers?

CHRYSALE.

Well . . . Trissotin.

ARISTE.

What! That ass, that figure of fun—

CHRYSALE.

Who babbles verse and Latin? Yes, that's the one.

ARISTE.

Did you agree to him?

CHRYSALE.

I? No; God forbid!

ARISTE.

What did you say, then?

CHRYSALE.

Nothing; and what I did
Was wise, I think, for it left me uncommitted.

ARISTE.

I see! What strategy! How nimble-witted!
Did you, at least, suggest Clitandre, Brother?

CHRYSALE.

No. When I found her partial toward another,
It seemed best not to push things then and there.

ARISTE.

Your prudence, truly, is beyond compare!
Aren't you ashamed to be so soft and meek?
How can a man be so absurdly weak
As to yield his wife an absolute dominion
And never dare contest her least opinion?

CHRYSALE.
Ah, Brother, that's easy enough for you to say.
You've no idea how noisy quarrels weigh
Upon my heart, which loves tranquillity,
And how my wife's bad temper frightens me.
Her nature's philosophic—or that's her claim,
But her tongue's sharp and savage all the same;
All this uplifting thought has not decreased
Her rancorous behavior in the least.
If I cross her even slightly, she will loose
An eight-day howling tempest of abuse.
There's no escape from her consuming ire;
She's like some frightful dragon spitting fire;
And yet, despite her devilish ways, my fear
Obliges me to call her "pet" and "dear."
ARISTE.
For shame. That's nonsense. It's your cowardice
Which lets your wife rule over you like this.
What power she has, your weakness has created;
She only rules because you've abdicated;
She couldn't bully you unless you chose,
Like an ass, to let her lead you by the nose.
Come now: despite your timid nature, can
You not resolve for once to be a man,
And, saying "This is how it's going to be,"
Lay down the law, and make your wife agree?
Shall you sacrifice your Henriette to these
Besotted women and their fantasies,
And take for son-in-law, and *heir*, a fool
Who's turned your house into a Latin-school,
A pedant whom your dazzled wife extols
As best of wits, most erudite of souls
And peerless fashioner of gallant verse,
And who, in all respects, could not be worse?
Once more I say, for shame: it's ludicrous
To see a husband cringe and cower thus.
CHRYSALE.
Yes, you're quite right; I see that I've been wrong.
It's high time, Brother, to be firm and strong,
To take a stand.

ARISTE.
                      Well said.
CHRYSALE.
                     It's base, I know,
To let a woman dominate one so.
ARISTE.
Quite right.
CHRYSALE.
             She's taken advantage of my patience.
ARISTE.
She has.
CHRYSALE.
            And of my peaceful inclinations.
ARISTE.
That's true.
CHRYSALE.
             But, as she'll learn this very day,
My daughter's mine, and I shall have my way
And wed her to a man who pleases me.
ARISTE.
Now you're the master, as I'd have you be.
CHRYSALE.
Brother, as young Clitandre's spokesman, you
Know where to find him. Send him to me, do.
ARISTE.
I'll go this instant.
CHRYSALE.
              Too long my will's been crossed;
Henceforth I'll be a man, whatever the cost.

ACT THREE

Scene 1

Philaminte, Armande, Bélise, Trissotin, Lépine

PHILAMINTE.
Let's all sit down and savor, thought by thought,
The verses which our learnèd guest has brought.
ARMANDE.
I burn to see them.
BÉLISE.
                    Yes; our souls are panting.
PHILAMINTE. (*To Trissotin.*)
All that your mind brings forth, I find enchanting.
ARMANDE.
For me, your compositions have no peer.
BÉLISE.
Their music is a banquet to my ear.
PHILAMINTE.
Don't tantalize your breathless audience.
ARMANDE.
Do hurry—
BÉLISE.
                    And relieve this sweet suspense.
PHILAMINTE.
Yield to our urging; give us your epigram.
TRISSOTIN. (*To Philaminte.*)
Madam, 'tis but an infant; still, I am
In hopes that you may condescend to love it,
Since on your doorstep I was delivered of it.
PHILAMINTE.
Knowing its father, I can do no other.
TRISSOTIN.
Your kind approval, then, shall be its mother.
BÉLISE.
What wit he has!

Henriette, Philaminte, Armande, Bélise, Trissotin, Lépine

PHILAMINTE. (*To Henriette, who has entered and has turned at once to go.*)
                    Ho! Don't rush off like that.
HENRIETTE.
I feared I might disrupt your pleasant chat.
PHILAMINTE.
Come here, and pay attention, and you shall share
The joy of hearing something rich and rare.
HENRIETTE.
I'm no fit judge of elegance in letters;
I leave such heady pastimes to my betters.
PHILAMINTE.
That doesn't matter. Stay, and when we're through
I shall reveal a sweet surprise to you.
TRISSOTIN. (*To Henriette.*)
What need you know of learning and the arts,
Who know so well the way to charm men's hearts?
HENRIETTE.
Sir, I know neither; nor is it my ambition—
BÉLISE.
Oh, please! Let's hear the infant composition.
PHILAMINTE. (*To Lépine.*)
Quick, boy, some chairs.
            (*Lépine falls down in bringing a chair.*)
                    Dear God, how loutish! Ought you
To fall like that, considering what we've taught you
Regarding equilibrium and its laws?
BÉLISE.
Look what you've done, fool. Surely you see the cause?
It was by wrongly shifting what we call
The center of gravity, that you came to fall.
LÉPINE.
I saw that when I hit the floor, alas.
PHILAMINTE. (*To Lépine, as he leaves.*)
Dolt!

TRISSOTIN.

It's a blessing he's not made of glass.

ARMANDE.

What wit! It never falters!

BÉLISE.

Not in the least.

(*All sit down.*)

PHILAMINTE.

Now then, do serve us your poetic feast.

TRISSOTIN.

For such great hunger as confronts me here,
An eight-line dish would not suffice, I fear.
My epigram's too slight. It would be wiser,
I think, to give you first, as appetizer,
A sonnet which a certain princess found
Subtle in sense, delectable in sound.
I've seasoned it with Attic salt throughout,
And you will find it tasty, I have no doubt.

ARMANDE.

How could we not?

PHILAMINTE.

Let's listen, with concentration.

BÉLISE. (*Interrupting Trissotin each time he starts to read.*)
My heart is leaping with anticipation.
I'm mad for poetry, and I love it best
When pregnant thoughts are gallantly expressed.

PHILAMINTE.

So long as we talk, our guest can't say a word.

TRISSOTIN.

SON—

BÉLISE. (*To Henriette.*)

Niece, be silent.

ARMANDE.

Please! Let the poem be heard.

TRISSOTIN.

SONNET TO THE PRINCESS URANIE, REGARDING HER FEVER

Your prudence, Madam, must have drowsed
When you took in so hot a foe
And let him be so nobly housed,
And feasted and regaled him so.

36

BÉLISE.
A fine first quatrain!
ARMANDE.

                    And the style! How gallant!
PHILAMINTE.
For metric flow he has a matchless talent.
ARMANDE.
"Your *prudence* must have *drowsed:*" a charming touch.
BÉLISE.
"So hot a foe" delights me quite as much.
PHILAMINTE.
I think that "feasted and regaled" conveys
A sense of richness in so many ways.
BÉLISE.
Let's listen to the rest.
TRISSOTIN.

            Your prudence, Madam, must have drowsed
            When you took in so hot a foe
            And let him be so nobly housed,
            And feasted and regaled him so.

ARMANDE.
"Your prudence must have drowsed!"
BÉLISE.
"So hot a foe!"
PHILAMINTE.
"Feasted and regaled!"
TRISSOTIN.

            Say what they may, the wretch must go!
            From your rich lodging drive away
            This ingrate who, as well you know,
            Would make your precious life his prey.

BÉLISE.
Oh! Pause a moment, I beg you; one is breathless.
ARMANDE.
Let us digest those verses, which are deathless.
PHILAMINTE.
There's a rare something in those lines which captures
One's inmost heart, and stirs the soul to raptures.

ARMANDE.

> "Say what they may, the wretch must go!
> From your rich lodging drive away . . ."

How apt that is— "rich lodging." I adore
The wit and freshness of that metaphor!
PHILAMINTE.

> "Say what they may, the wretch must go!"

That "Say what they may" is greatly to my liking.
I've never encountered any words more striking.
ARMANDE.
Nor I. That "Say what they may" bewitches me.
BÉLISE.
"Say what they may" is brilliant, I agree.
ARMANDE.
Oh, to have said it.
BÉLISE.

> It's a whole poem in a phrase.

PHILAMINTE.
But have you fully grasped what it conveys,
As I have?
ARMANDE and BÉLISE.

> Oh! Oh!

PHILAMINTE.

> "Say what they may, the wretch must go!"

That means, if people take the fever's side,
Their pleadings should be scornfully denied.

> "Say what they may, the wretch must go,
> Say what they may, say what they may!"

There's more in that "Say what they may" than first appears.
Perhaps I am alone in this, my dears,
But I see no limit to what that phrase implies.
BÉLISE.
It's true, it means a great deal for its size.
PHILAMINTE. (*To Trissotin.*)
Sir, when you wrote this charming "Say what they may,"
Did you know your own great genius? Can you say
That you were conscious, then, of all the wit
And wealth of meaning we have found in it?
TRISSOTIN.
Ah! Well!

ARMANDE.
>I'm very fond of "ingrate," too.
It well describes that villain fever, who
Repays his hosts by causing them distress.

PHILAMINTE.
In short, the quatrains are a great success.
Do let us have the tercets now, I pray.

ARMANDE.
Oh, please, let's once more hear "Say what they may."

TRISSOTIN.
>Say what they may, the wretch must go!

PHILAMINTE, ARMANDE and BÉLISE.
"Say what they may!"

TRISSOTIN.
>From your rich lodging drive away . . .

PHILAMINTE, ARMANDE and BÉLISE.
"Rich lodging!"

TRISSOTIN.
>This ingrate who, as well you know . . .

PHILAMINTE, ARMANDE and BÉLISE.
That "ingrate" of a fever!

TRISSOTIN.
>Would make your precious life his prey.

PHILAMINTE.
"Your precious life!"

ARMANDE and BÉLISE.
Ah!

TRISSOTIN.
>What! Shall he mock your rank, and pay
>No deference to the blood of kings?

PHILAMINTE, ARMANDE and BÉLISE.
Ah!

TRISSOTIN.
>Shall he afflict you night and day,
>And shall you tolerate such things?
>No! To the baths you must repair,
>And with your own hands drown him there.

PHILAMINTE.
I'm overcome.

BÉLISE.
                              I'm faint.
ARMANDE.
                                        I'm ravished, quite.
PHILAMINTE.
One feels a thousand tremors of delight.
ARMANDE.
              "And shall you tolerate such things?"
BÉLISE.
              "No! To the baths you must repair . . ."
PHILAMINTE.
              "And with your own hands drown him there."
Drown, him, that is to say, in the bath-water.
ARMANDE.
Your verse, at each step, gives some glad surprise.
BÉLISE.
Wherever one turns, fresh wonders greet the eyes.
PHILAMINTE.
One treads on beauty, wandering through your lines.
ARMANDE.
They're little paths all strewn with eglantines.
TRISSOTIN.
You find the poem, then—
PHILAMINTE.
                              Perfect, and, what's more,
Novel: the like was never done before.
BÉLISE. (*To Henriette.*)
What, Niece, did not this reading stir your heart?
By saying nothing, you've played a dreary part.
HENRIETTE.
We play what parts we're given, here below;
Wishing to be a wit won't make one so.
TRISSOTIN.
Perhaps my verses bored her.
HENRIETTE.
                              No indeed;
I didn't listen.
PHILAMINTE.
                  The epigram! Please proceed.

TRISSOTIN.

CONCERNING A VERMILION COACH, GIVEN TO A LADY OF
HIS ACQUAINTANCE . . .

PHILAMINTE.

There's always something striking about his titles.

ARMANDE.

They ready us for the wit of his recitals.

TRISSOTIN.

        Love sells his bonds to me at such a rate . . .

PHILAMINTE, ARMANDE and BÉLISE.

Ah!

TRISSOTIN.

    I've long since spent the half of my estate;
      And when you see this coach, embossed
      With heavy gold at such a cost
      That all the dazzled countryside
    Gapes as my Laïs passes in her pride . . .

PHILAMINTE.

Listen to that. "My Laïs." How erudite!

BÉLISE.

A stunning reference. So exactly right.

TRISSOTIN.

      And when you see this coach, embossed
      With heavy gold at such a cost
      That all the dazzled countryside
    Gapes as my Laïs passes in her pride,
      Know by that vision of vermilion
      That what was mine is now *her* million.

ARMANDE.

Oh! Oh! I didn't foresee that final twist.

PHILAMINTE.

We have no subtler epigrammatist.

BÉLISE.

      "Know by that vision of vermilion
      That what was mine is now *her* million."

The rhyme is clever, and yet not forced: "*vermilion, her*
                        million."

PHILAMINTE.

Since first we met, Sir, I have had the highest

Opinion of you; it may be that I'm biased;
But all you write, to my mind, stands alone.
TRISSOTIN. (*To Philaminte.*)
If you'd but read us something of your own,
One might reciprocate your admiration.
PHILAMINTE.
I've no new poems, but it's my expectation
That soon, in some eight chapters, you may see
The plans I've made for our Academy.
Plato, in his *Republic*, did not go
Beyond an abstract outline, as you know,
But what I've shaped in words, I shall not fail
To realize, in most concrete detail.
I'm much offended by the disrespect
Which men display for women's intellect,
And I intend to avenge us, every one,
For all the slighting things which men have done—
Assigning us to cares which stunt our souls,
And banning our pursuit of studious goals.
ARMANDE.
It's too insulting to forbid our sex
To ponder any questions more complex
Than whether some lace is pretty, or some brocade,
And whether a skirt or cloak is nicely made.
BÉLISE.
It's time we broke our mental chains, and stated
Our high intent to be emancipated.
TRISSOTIN.
My deep respect for women none can deny;
Though I may praise a lady's lustrous eye,
I honor, too, the lustre of her mind.
PHILAMINTE.
For that, you have the thanks of womankind;
But there are some proud scholars I could mention
To whom we'll prove, despite their condescension,
That women may be learned if they please,
And found, like men, their own academies.
Ours, furthermore, shall be more wisely run
Than theirs: we'll roll all disciplines into one,
Uniting letters, in a rich alliance,
With all the tools and theories of science,

And in our thought refusing to be thrall
To any school, but making use of all.
TRISSOTIN.
For method, Aristotle suits me well.
PHILAMINTE.
But in abstractions, Plato *does* excel.
ARMANDE.
The thought of Epicurus is very keen.
BÉLISE.
I rather like his atoms, but as between
A vacuum and a field of subtle matter
I find it easier to accept the latter.
TRISSOTIN.
On magnetism, Descartes supports my notions.
ARMANDE.
I love his falling worlds . . .
PHILAMINTE.

                     And whirling motions!
ARMANDE.
I can't wait for our conclaves. We shall proclaim
Discoveries, and they shall bring us fame.
TRISSOTIN.
Yes, to your keen minds Nature can but yield,
And let her rarest secrets be revealed.
PHILAMINTE.
I can already offer one such rarity:
I have seen men in the moon, with perfect clarity.
BÉLISE.
I'm not sure I've seen men, but I can say
That I've seen steeples there, as plain as day.
ARMANDE.
To master grammar and physics is our intent,
And history, ethics, verse, and government.
PHILAMINTE.
Ethics, which thrills me in so many respects,
Was once the passion of great intellects;
But it's the Stoics to whom I'd give the prize;
They knew that only the virtuous can be wise.
ARMANDE.
Regarding language, we aim to renovate
Our tongue through laws which soon we'll promulgate.

Each of us has conceived a hatred, based
On outraged reason or offended taste,
For certain nouns and verbs. We've gathered these
Into a list of shared antipathies,
And shall proceed to doom and banish them.
At each of our learned gatherings, we'll condemn
In mordant terms those words which we propose
To purge from usage, whether in verse or prose.
PHILAMINTE.
But our academy's noblest plan of action,
A scheme in which I take deep satisfaction,
A glorious project which will earn the praise
Of all discerning minds of future days,
Is to suppress those *syllables* which, though found
In blameless words, may have a shocking sound,
Which naughty punsters utter with a smirk,
Which, age on age, coarse jesters overwork,
And which, by filthy double-meanings, vex
The finer feelings of the female sex.
TRISSOTIN.
You have most wondrous plans, beyond a doubt!
BÉLISE.
You'll see our by-laws, once we've worked them out.
TRISSOTIN.
They can't fail to be beautiful and wise.
ARMANDE.
By our high standards we shall criticize
Whatever's written, and be severe with it.
We'll show that only we and our friends have wit.
We'll search out faults in everything, while citing
Ourselves alone for pure and flawless writing.

SCENE 3

Lépine, Trissotin, Philaminte, Bélise, Armande, Henriette, Vadius

LÉPINE. (*To Trissotin.*)
There's a man outside to see you, Sir; he's wearing
Black, and he has a gentle voice and bearing.
                    (*All rise.*)

TRISSOTIN.
It's that learnèd friend of mine, who's begged me to
Procure for him the honor of meeting you.
PHILAMINTE.
Please have him enter; you have our full consent.

(*Trissotin goes to admit Vadius, Philaminte speaks to Armande and Bélise.*)

We must be gracious, and most intelligent.

(*To Henriette, who seeks to leave.*)

Whoa, there! I told you plainly, didn't I,
That I wished you to remain with us?
HENRIETTE.

But why?

PHILAMINTE.
Come back, and you shall shortly understand.
TRISSOTIN. (*Returning with Vadius.*)
Behold a man who yearns to kiss your hand;
And in presenting him, I have no fear
That he'll profane this cultured atmosphere:
Among our choicest wits, he quite stands out.
PHILAMINTE.
Since you present him, his worth's beyond a doubt.
TRISSOTIN.
In classics, he's the greatest of savants,
And knows more Greek than any man in France.
PHILAMINTE. (*To Bélise.*)
Greek! Sister, our guest knows Greek! How marvelous!
BÉLISE. (*To Armande.*)
Greek, Niece! Do you hear?
ARMANDE.

Yes, Greek! What joy for us!

PHILAMINTE.
Think of it! Greek! Oh, Sir, for the love of Greek,
Permit us each to kiss you on the cheek.

(*Vadius kisses them all save Henriette, who refuses.*)

HENRIETTE.
I don't know Greek, Sir; permit me to decline.
PHILAMINTE.
I think Greek books are utterly divine.
VADIUS.
In my eagerness to meet you, I fear I've come

Intruding on some grave symposium.
Forgive me, Madam, if I've caused confusion.
PHILAMINTE.
Ah, Sir, to bring us Greek is no intrusion.
TRISSOTIN.
My friend does wonders, too, in verse and prose,
And might well show us something, if he chose.
VADIUS.
The fault of authors is their inclination
To dwell upon their works in conversation,
And whether in parks, or parlors, or at table,
To spout their poems as often as they're able.
How sad to see a writer play the extorter,
Demanding oh's and ah's from every quarter,
And forcing any gathering whatever
To tell him that his labored verse is clever.
I've never embraced the folly of which I speak,
And hold the doctrine of a certain Greek
That men of sense, however well endowed,
Should shun the urge to read their works aloud.
Still, here are some lines, concerning youthful love,
Which I'd be pleased to hear your judgments of.
TRISSOTIN.
For verve and beauty, your verses stand alone.
VADIUS.
Venus and all the Graces grace your own.
TRISSOTIN.
Your choice of words is splendid, and your phrasing.
VADIUS.
Your *ethos* and your *pathos* are amazing.
TRISSOTIN.
The polished eclogues which you've given us
Surpass both Virgil and Theocritus.
VADIUS.
Your odes are noble, gallant, and refined,
And leave your master Horace far behind.
TRISSOTIN.
Ah, but your little love-songs: what could be sweeter?
VADIUS.
As for your well-turned sonnets, none are neater.

46

TRISSOTIN.
Your deft *rondeaux*, are any poems more charming?
VADIUS.
Your madrigals—are any more disarming?
TRISSOTIN.
Above all, you're a wizard at *ballades*.
VADIUS.
At *bouts-rimés*, you always have the odds.
TRISSOTIN.
If France would only recognize your merits—
VADIUS.
If the age did justice to its finer spirits—
TRISSOTIN.
You'd have a gilded coach in which to ride.
VADIUS.
Statues of you would rise on every side.
                    (*To Trissotin.*)
Hem! Now for my *ballade*. Please comment on it
In the frankest—
TRISSOTIN.

                              Have you seen a certain sonnet
About the fever of Princess Uranie?
VADIUS.
Yes. It was read to me yesterday, at tea.
TRISSOTIN.
Do you know who wrote it?
VADIUS.

                              No, but of this I'm sure:
The sonnet, frankly, is very, very poor.
TRISSOTIN.
Oh? Many people have praised it, nonetheless.
VADIUS.
That doesn't prevent its being a sorry mess,
And if you've read it, I know you share my view.
TRISSOTIN.
Why no, I don't in the least agree with you;
Not many sonnets boast so fine a style.
VADIUS.
God grant I never write a thing so vile!

47

TRISSOTIN.
It couldn't be better written, I contend;
And I should know, because I wrote it, friend.
VADIUS.
You?
TRISSOTIN.
       I.
VADIUS.
                  Well, how this happened I can't explain.
TRISSOTIN.
What happened was that you found my poem inane.
VADIUS.
When I heard the sonnet, I must have been distrait;
Or perhaps 't'was read in an unconvincing way.
But let's forget it; this *ballade* of mine—
TRISSOTIN.
Ballades, I think, are rather asinine.
The form's old-hat; it has a musty smell.
VADIUS.
Still, many people like it very well.
TRISSOTIN.
That doesn't prevent my finding it dull and flat.
VADIUS.
No, but the form is none the worse for that.
TRISSOTIN.
The *ballade* is dear to pedants; they adore it.
VADIUS.
How curious, then, that you should not be for it.
TRISSOTIN.
You see in others your own drab qualities.
                (*All rise.*)
VADIUS.
Don't see your own in me, Sir, if you please.
TRISSOTIN.
Be off, you jingling dunce! Let's end this session.
VADIUS.
You scribbler! You disgrace to the profession!
TRISSOTIN.
You poetaster! You shameless plagiarist!

48

VADIUS.
You ink-stained thief!
PHILAMINTE.

Oh, gentlemen! Please desi:
TRISSOTIN. (*To Vadius.*)
Go to the greeks and Romans, and pay back
The thousand things you've filched from them, you hack.
VADIUS.
Go to Parnassus and confess your guilt
For turning Horace into a crazy-quilt.
TRISSOTIN.
Think of your book, which caused so little stir.
VADIUS.
And you, Sir, think of your bankrupt publisher.
TRISSOTIN.
My fame's established; in vain you mock me so.
VADIUS.
Do tell. Go look at the *Satires* of Boileau.
TRISSOTIN.
Go look at them yourself.
VADIUS.

As between us two,
I'm treated there more honorably than you.
He gives me a passing thrust, and links my name
With several authors of no little fame;
But nowhere do his verses leave you in peace;
His witty attacks upon you never cease.
TRISSOTIN.
It's therefore I whom he respects the more.
To him, you're one of the crowd, a minor bore;
You're given a single sword-thrust, and are reckoned
Too insignificant to deserve a second.
But me he singles out as a noble foe
Against whom he must strive with blow on blow,
Betraying, by those many strokes, that he
Is never certain of the victory.
VADIUS.
My pen will teach you that I'm no poetaster.
TRISSOTIN.
And mine will show you, fool, that I'm your master.

VADIUS.
I challenge you in verse, prose, Latin, and Greek.
TRISSOTIN.
We'll meet at Barbin's bookshop, in a week.

SCENE 4

Trissotin, Philaminte, Armande, Bélise, Henriette

TRISSOTIN. (*To Philaminte.*)
Forgive me if my wrath grew uncontrolled;
I felt an obligation to uphold
Your judgment of that sonnet he maligned.
PHILAMINTE.
I'll try to mend your quarrel; never mind.
Let's change the subject. Henriette, come here.
I've long been troubled because you don't appear
At all endowed with wit or intellect;
But I've a remedy, now, for that defect.
HENRIETTE.
Don't trouble, Mother; I wish no remedy.
Learnèd discourse is not my cup of tea.
I like to take life easy, and I balk
At trying to be a fount of clever talk.
I've no ambition to be a parlor wit,
And if I'm stupid, I don't mind a bit.
I'd rather speak in a plain and common way
Than rack my brains for brilliant things to say.
PHILAMINTE.
I know your shameful tastes, which I decline
To countenance in any child of mine.
Beauty of face is but a transient flower,
A brief adornment, the glory of an hour,
And goes no deeper than the outer skin;
But beauty of mind endures, and lies within.
I've long sought means to cultivate in you
A beauty such as time could not undo,
And plant within your breast a noble yearning
For higher knowledge and the fruits of learning;

And now, at last, I've settled on a plan,
Which is to mate you with a learnèd man—
     (*Gesturing toward Trissotin.*)
This gentleman, in short, whom I decree
Than you acknowledge as your spouse-to-be.
HENRIETTE.
I, Mother?
PHILAMINTE.
     Yes, you. Stop playing innocent.
BÉLISE. (*To Trissotin.*)
I understand. Your eyes ask my consent
Before you pledge to her a heart that's mine.
Do so. All claims I willingly resign:
This match will bring you wealth and happiness.
TRISSOTIN. (*To Henriette.*)
My rapture, Madam, is more than I can express:
The honor which this marriage will confer
Upon me—
HENRIETTE.
    Hold! It's not yet settled, Sir;
Don't rush things.
PHILAMINTE.
     What a reply! How overweening!
Girl, if you dare . . . Enough, you take my meaning.
     (*To Trissotin.*)
Just let her be. Her mind will soon be changed.

SCENE 5

Henriette, Armande

ARMANDE.
What a brilliant match our mother has arranged!
She's found for you a spouse both great and wise.
HENRIETTE.
Why don't you take him, if he's such a prize?
ARMANDE.
It's you, not I, who are to be his bride.

51

HENRIETTE.
For my elder sister, I'll gladly step aside.
ARMANDE.
If I, like you, yearned for the wedded state,
I'd take your offer of so fine a mate.
HENRIETTE.
If I, like you, were charmed by pedantry,
I'd think the man a perfect choice for me.
ARMANDE.
Our tastes may differ, Sister, but we still
Owe strict obedience to our parents' will;
Whether or not you're fractious and contrary,
You'll wed the man our mother bids you marry . . .

SCENE 6

Chrysale, Ariste, Clitandre, Henriette, Armande

CHRYSALE. (*To Henriette, presenting Clitandre.*)
Now, Daughter, you shall do as I command.
Take off that glove, and give this man your hand,
And think of him henceforward as the one
I've chosen as your husband and my son.
ARMANDE.
In this case, Sister, you're easy to persuade.
HENRIETTE.
Sister, our parents' will must be obeyed;
I'll wed the man my father bids me marry.
ARMANDE.
Your mother's blessing, too, is necessary.
CHRYSALE.
Just what do you mean?
ARMANDE.
               I much regret to state
That Mother has a rival candidate
For the hand of Henri—
CHRYSALE.
               Hush, you chatterer!
Go prate about philosophy with her,

52

And cease to meddle in what is my affair.
Tell her it's settled, and bid her to beware
Of angering me by making any fuss.
Go on, now.
ARISTE.

                              Bràvo! This is miraculous.
CLITANDRE.
How fortunate I am! What bliss! What joy!
CHRYSALE. (*To Clitandre.*)
Come, take her hand, now. After you, my boy;
Conduct her to her room. (*To Ariste.*) Ah, Brother, this is
A tonic to me; think of those hugs, those kisses!
It warms my old heart, and reminds me of
My youthful days of gallantry and love.

ACT FOUR

Scene 1

Armande, Philaminte

ARMANDE.
Oh, no, she didn't waver or delay,
But, with a flourish, hastened to obey.
Almost before he spoke, she had agreed
To do his bidding, and she appeared, indeed,
Moved by defiance toward her mother, rather
Than deference to the wishes of her father.
PHILAMINTE.
I soon shall show her to whose government
The laws of reason oblige her to consent,
And whether it's matter or form, body or soul,
Father or mother, who is in control.
ARMANDE.
The least they could have done was to consult you;
It's graceless of that young man to insult you
By trying to wed your child without your blessing.
PHILAMINTE.
He's not yet won. His looks are prepossessing,
And I approved his paying court to you;
But I never liked his manners. He well knew
That writing poetry is a gift of mine,
And yet he never asked to hear a line.

Scene 2

Clitandre, *entering quietly and listening unseen,* **Armande,**

Philaminte

ARMANDE.
Mother, if I were you, I shouldn't let
That gentleman espouse our Henriette.

Not that I care, of course; I do not speak
As someone moved by prejudice or pique,
Or by a heart which, having been forsaken,
Asks vengeance for the wounds which it has taken.
For what I've suffered, philosophy can give
Full consolation, helping one to live
On a high plane, and treat such things with scorn;
But what he's done to you can not be borne.
Honor requires that you oppose his suit;
Besides, you'd never come to like the brute.
In all our talks, I cannot recollect
His speaking of you with the least respect.
PHILAMINTE.
Young whelp!
ARMANDE.
                    Despite your work's great reputation,
He icily withheld his approbation.
PHILAMINTE.
The churl!
ARMANDE.
                    A score of times, I read to him
Your latest poems. He tore them limb from limb.
PHILAMINTE.
The beast!
ARMANDE.
                    We quarreled often about your writing,
And you would not believe how harsh, how biting—
CLITANDRE. (*To Armande.*)
Ah, Madam, a little charity, I pray,
Or a little truthful speaking, anyway.
How have I wronged you? What was the offense
Which makes you seek, by slanderous eloquence,
To rouse against me the distaste and ire
Of those whose good opinion I require?
Speak, Madam, and justify your vicious grudge.
I'll gladly let your mother be our judge.
ARMANDE.
Had I the grudge of which I stand accused,
I could defend it, for I've been ill-used.
First love, Sir, is a pure and holy flame

Which makes upon us an eternal claim;
'T'were better to renounce this world, and die,
Than be untrue to such a sacred tie.
Fickleness is a monstrous crime, and in
The moral scale there is no heavier sin.
CLITANDRE.
Do you call it fickleness, *Madame*, to do
What your heart's cold disdain has driven me to?
If, by submitting to its cruel laws,
I've wounded you, your own proud heart's the cause.
My love for you was fervent and entire;
For two whole years it burned with constant fire;
My duty, care, and worship did not falter;
I laid my heart's devotion on your altar.
But all my love and service were in vain;
You dashed the hopes I dared to entertain.
If, thus rejected, I made overtures
To someone else, was that my fault, or yours?
Was I inconstant, or was I forced to be?
Did I forsake you, or did you banish me?
ARMANDE.
Sir, can you say that I've refused your love
When all I've sought has been to purge it of
Vulgarity, and teach you that refined
And perfect passion which is of the mind?
Can you not learn an ardor which dispenses
Entirely with the commerce of the senses,
Or see how sweetly spirits may be blended
When bodily desires have been transcended?
Alas, your love is carnal, and cannot rise
Above the plane of gross material ties;
The flame of your devotion can't be fed
Except by marriage, and the marriage-bed.
How strange is such a love! And oh, how far
Above such earthliness true lovers are!
In their delights, the body plays no part,
And their clear flames but marry heart to heart,
Rejecting all the rest as low and bestial.
Their fire is pure, unsullied, and celestial.
The sighs they breathe are blameless, and express

No filthy hankerings, no fleshliness.
There's no ulterior goal they hunger for.
They love for love's sake, and for nothing more,
And since the spirit is their only care,
Bodies are things of which they're unaware.
CLITANDRE.
Well, I'm aware, though you may blush to hear it,
That I have both a body and a spirit;
Nor can I part them to my satisfaction;
I fear I lack the power of abstraction
Whereby such philosophic feats are done,
And so my body and soul must live as one.
There's nothing finer, as you say, than these
Entirely spiritual ecstasies,
These marriages of souls, these sentiments
So purified of any taint of sense;
But such love is, for my taste, too ethereal;
I am, as you've complained, a bit material;
I love with all my being, and I confess
That a whole woman is what I would possess.
Need I be damned for feelings of the kind?
With all respect for your high views, I find
That men in general feel my sort of passion,
That marriage still is pretty much in fashion,
And that it's deemed an honorable estate;
So that my asking you to be my mate,
And share with me that good and sweet condition,
Was scarcely an indecent proposition.
ARMANDE.
Ah well, Sir: since you thrust my views aside,
Since your brute instincts must be satisfied,
And since your feelings, to be faithful, must
Be bound by ties of flesh and chains of lust,
I'll force myself, if Mother will consent,
To grant the thing on which you're so intent.
CLITANDRE.
It's too late, Madam: another's occupied
Your place; if I now took you as my bride,
I'd wrong a heart which sheltered and consoled me
When, in your pride, you'd treated me so coldly.

57

PHILAMINTE.
Sir, do you dream of my consenting to
This other marriage which you have in view?
Does it not penetrate your mind as yet
That I have other plans for Henriette?
CLITANDRE.
Ah, Madam, reconsider, if you please,
And don't expose me thus to mockeries;
Don't put me in the ludicrous position
Of having Trissotin for competition.
What a shabby rival! You couldn't have selected
A wit less honored, a pedant less respected.
We've many pseudo-wits and polished frauds
Whose cleverness the time's bad taste applauds,
But Trissotin fools no one, and indeed
His writings are abhorred by all who read.
Save in this house, his work is never praised,
And I have been repeatedly amazed
To hear you laud some piece of foolishness
Which, had you written it, you would suppress.
PHILAMINTE.
That's how you judge him. We feel otherwise
Because we look at him with different eyes.

SCENE 3

Trissotin, Armande, Philaminte, Clitandre

TRISSOTIN. (*To Philaminte.*)
I bring you, Madam, some startling news I've heard.
Last night, a near-catastrophe occurred:
While we were all asleep, a comet crossed
Our vortex, and the Earth was all but lost;
Had it collided with our world, alas,
We'd have been shattered into bits, like glass.
PHILAMINTE.
Let's leave that subject for another time;
This gentleman, I fear, would see no rhyme
Or reason in it; it's ignorance he prizes;
Learning and wit are things which he despises.

CLITANDRE.
Kindly permit me, Madam, to restate
Your summary of my views: I only hate
Such wit and learning as twist men's brains awry.
Those things are excellent in themselves, but I
Had rather be an ignorant man, by far,
Than learnèd in the way some people are.
TRISSOTIN.
Well, as for me, I hold that learning never
Could twist a man in any way whatever.
CLITANDRE.
And I assert that learning often breeds
Men who are foolish both in words and deeds.
TRISSOTIN.
What a striking paradox!
CLITANDRE.
                        Though I'm no wit,
I'd have no trouble, I think, in proving it.
If arguments should fail, I'm sure I'd find
That living proofs came readily to mind.
TRISSOTIN.
The living proofs you gave might not persuade.
CLITANDRE.
I'd not look far before my point was made.
TRISSOTIN.
I cannot think, myself, of such a case.
CLITANDRE.
I can; indeed, it stares me in the face.
TRISSOTIN.
I thought it was by ignorance, and not
By learning, Sir, that great fools were begot.
CLITANDRE.
Well, you thought wrongly. It's a well-known rule
That no fool's greater than a learnèd fool.
TRISSOTIN.
Our common usage contradicts that claim,
Since "fool" and "ignoramus" mean the same.
CLITANDRE.
You think those words synonymous? Oh no, Sir!
You'll find that "fool" and "pedant" are much closer.

TRISSOTIN.
"Fool" denotes plain and simple foolishness.
CLITANDRE.
"Pedant" denotes the same, in fancy dress.
TRISSOTIN.
The quest for knowledge is noble and august.
CLITANDRE.
But knowledge, in a pedant, turns to dust.
TRISSOTIN.
It's clear that ignorance has great charms for you,
Or else you wouldn't defend it as you do.
CLITANDRE.
I came to see the charms of ignorance when
I made the acquaintance of certain learnèd men.
TRISSOTIN.
Those certain learnèd men, it may turn out,
Are better than certain folk who strut about.
CLITANDRE.
The learnèd men would say so, certainly;
But then, those certain folk might not agree.
PHILAMINTE. (To Clitandre.)
I think, Sir—
CLITANDRE.
          Madam, spare me, please. This rough
Assailant is already fierce enough.
Don't join him, pray, in giving me a beating.
I shall preserve myself, now, by retreating.
ARMANDE.
You, with your brutal taunts, were the offender;
'Twas you—
CLITANDRE.
          More reinforcements! I surrender.
PHILAMINTE.
Sir, witty repartee is quite all right,
But personal attacks are impolite.
CLITANDRE.
Good Lord, he's quite unhurt, as one can tell.
No one in France takes ridicule so well.
For years he's heard men gibe at him, and scoff,
And in his smugness merely laughed it off.

TRISSOTIN.

I'm not surprised to hear this gentleman say
The things he's said in this unpleasant fray.
He's much at court, and as one might expect,
He shares the court's mistrust of intellect,
And, as a courtier, defends with zest
The ignorance that's in its interest.

CLITANDRE.

You're very hard indeed on the poor court,
Which hears each day how people of your sort,
Who deal in intellectual wares, decry it,
Complain that their careers are blighted by it,
Deplore its wretched taste, and blame their own
Unhappy failures on that cause alone.
Permit me, Mister Trissotin, with due
Respect for your great name, to say that you
And all your kind would do well to discuss
The court in tones less harsh and querulous;
That the court is not so short of wit and brain
As you and all your scribbling friends maintain;
That all things, there, are viewed with common sense,
That good taste, too, is much in evidence,
And that its knowledge of the world surpasses
The fusty learning of pedantic asses.

TRISSOTIN.

It has good taste, you say? If only it had!

CLITANDRE.

What makes you say, Sir, that its taste is bad?

TRISSOTIN.

What makes me say so? Rasiùs and Baldùs
Do France great honor by what their pens produce,
Yet the court pays these scholars no attention,
And neither of them has received a pension.

CLITANDRE.

I now perceive your grievance, and I see
That you've left your own name out, from modesty.
Well, let's not drag it into our debate.
Just tell me: how have your heroes served the State?
What are their writings worth, that they expect
Rewards, and charge the nation with neglect?

Why should they whine, these learnèd friends of yours,
At not receiving gifts and sinecures?
A precious lot they've done for France, indeed!
Their tomes are just what court and country need!
The vanity of such beggars makes me laugh:
Because they're set in type and bound in calf,
They think that they're illustrious citizens;
That the fate of nations hangs upon their pens;
That the least mention of their work should bring
The pensions flocking in on eager wing;
That the whole universe, with one wide stare,
Admires them; that their fame is everywhere,
And that they're wondrous wise because they know
What others said before them, long ago;—
Because they've given thirty years of toil
And eye-strain to acquire, by midnight oil,
Some jumbled Latin and some garbled Greek,
And overload their brains with the antique
Obscurities which lie about in books.
These bookworms, with their smug, myopic looks,
Are full of pompous talk and windy unction;
They have no common sense, no useful function,
And could, in short, persuade the human race
To think all wit and learning a disgrace.
PHILAMINTE.
You speak most heatedly, and it is clear
What feelings prompt you to be so severe;
Your rival's presence, which seems to irk you greatly—

SCENE 4

Julien, Trissotin, Philaminte, Clitandre, Armande

JULIEN.
The learnèd man who visited you lately,
And whose valet I have the honor to be,
Sends you this note, *Madame,* by way of me.
PHILAMINTE.
Whatever the import of this note you bring,
Do learn, my friend, that it's a graceless thing

To interrupt a conversation so,
And that a rightly-trained valet would go
To the servants first, and ask them for admission.
JULIEN.
Madam, I'll bear in mind your admonition.
PHILAMINTE. (*Reading.*)
    "Trissotin boasts, Madam, that he is going to marry
your daughter. Let me warn you that that great thinker
is thinking only of your wealth, and that you would do
well to put off the marriage until you have seen the poem
which I am now composing against him. It is to be a
portrait in verse, and I propose to depict him for you in
his true colors. Meanwhile, I am sending herewith the
works of Horace, Virgil, Terence, and Catullus, in the
margins of which I have marked, for your benefit, all the
passages which he has plundered."
Well, well! To thwart the match which I desire,
A troop of enemies have opened fire
Upon this worthy man; but I'll requite
By one swift action their dishonest spite,
And show them all that their combined assault
Has only hastened what they strove to halt.
            (*To Julien.*)
Take back those volumes to your master, and
Inform him, so that he'll clearly understand
Precisely how much value I have set
Upon his sage advice, that Henriette
            (*Pointing to Trissotin.*)
Shall wed this gentleman, this very night.
            (*To Clitandre.*)
Sir, you're a friend of the family. I invite
You most sincerely to remain and see
The contract signed, as shortly it shall be.
Armande, you'll send for the notary, and prepare
Your sister for her part in this affair.
ARMANDE.
No need for me to let my sister know;
This gentleman, I'm sure, will quickly go
To tell her all the news, and seek as well
To prompt her saucy spirit to rebel.

PHILAMINTE.
We'll see by whom her spirit will be swayed;
It doesn't suit me to be disobeyed.

SCENE 5

Armande, Clitandre

ARMANDE.
I'm very sorry for you, Sir; it seems
Things haven't gone according to your schemes.
CLITANDRE.
Madam, I mean to do my very best
To lift that weight of sorrow from your breast.
ARMANDE.
I fear, Sir, that your hopes are not well-grounded.
CLITANDRE.
It may be that your fear will prove ill-founded.
ARMANDE.
I hope so.
CLITANDRE.
              I believe you; nor do I doubt
That you'll do all you can to help me out.
ARMANDE.
To serve your cause shall be my sole endeavor.
CLITANDRE.
For that, you'll have my gratitude forever.

SCENE 6

Chrysale, Ariste, Henriette, Clitandre

CLITANDRE.
I shall be lost unless you help me, Sir:
Your wife's rejected my appeals to her,
And chosen Trissotin for her son-in-law.
CHRYSALE.
Damn it, what ails the woman? I never saw
What in this Trissotin could so attract her.

ARISTE.
He versifies in Latin, and that's a factor
Which makes him, in her view, the better man.
CLITANDRE.
To marry them tonight, Sir, is her plan.
CHRYSALE.
Tonight?
CLITANDRE.
       Tonight.
CHRYSALE.
            Her plan, then, will miscarry.
I promise that, tonight, you two shall marry.
CLITANDRE.
She's having a contract drawn by the notary.
CHRYSALE.
Well, he shall draw another one for me.
CLITANDRE. *(Indicating Henriette.)*
Armande has orders to inform this lady
Of the wedding-match for which she's to be ready.
CHRYSALE.
And I inform her that, by my command,
It's you on whom she shall bestow her hand.
This is my house, and I shall make it clear
That I'm the one and only master here.
           (To Henriette.)
Wait, Daughter; we'll join you when our errand's done.
Come, Brother, follow me; you too, my son.
HENRIETTE. *(To Ariste.)*
Please keep him in this mood, whatever you do.
ARISTE.
I'll do my utmost for your love and you.

SCENE 8

Henriette, Clitandre

CLITANDRE.
Whatever aid our kind allies may lend,
It's your true heart on which my hopes depend.

65

HENRIETTE.
As to my heart, of that you may be sure.
CLITANDRE.
If so, my own is happy and secure.
HENRIETTE.
I must be strong, so as not to be coerced.
CLITANDRE.
Cling to our love, and let them do their worst.
HENRIETTE.
I'll do my best to make our cause prevail;
But if my hope of being yours should fail,
And if it seems I'm to be forced to marry,
A convent cell shall be my sanctuary.
CLITANDRE.
Heaven grant that you need never give to me
Such painful proof of your fidelity.

ACT FIVE

SCENE 1

Henriette, Trissotin

HENRIETTE.
It seems to me that we two should confer
About this contemplated marriage, Sir,
Since it's reduced our household to dissension.
Do give my arguments your kind attention.
I know that you expect to realize,
By wedding me, a dowry of some size;
Yet money, which so many men pursue,
Should bore a true philosopher like you,
And your contempt for riches should be shown
In your behavior, not in words alone.
TRISSOTIN.
It's not in wealth that your attraction lies:
Your sparkling charms, your soft yet flashing eyes,
Your airs, your graces—it is these in which
My ravished heart perceives you to be rich,
These treasures only which I would possess.
HENRIETTE.
I'm honored by the love which you profess,
Although I can't see what I've done to earn it,
And much regret, Sir, that I can't return it.
I have the highest estimation of you,
But there's one reason why I cannot love you.
A heart's devotion cannot be divided,
And it's Clitandre on whom my heart's decided.
I know he lacks your merits, which are great,
That I'm obtuse to choose him for my mate,
That you should please me by your gifts and wit;
I know I'm wrong, but there's no help for it;
Though reason chides me for my want of sense,
My heart clings blindly to its preference.

TRISSOTIN.
When I am given your hand and marriage-vow,
I'll claim the heart Clitandre possesses now,
And I dare hope that I can then incline
That heart, by sweet persuasions, to be mine.
HENRIETTE.
No, no: first love, Sir, is too strong a feeling.
All your persuasions could not prove appealing.
Let me, upon this point, be blunt and plain,
Since nothing I shall say could cause you pain.
The fires of love, which set our hearts aglow,
Aren't kindled by men's merits, as you know.
They're most capricious; when someone takes our eye,
We're often quite unable to say why.
If, Sir, our loves were based on wise selection,
You would have all my heart, all my affection;
But love quite clearly doesn't work that way.
Indulge me in my blindness, then, I pray,
And do not show me, Sir, so little mercy
As to desire that others should coerce me.
What man of honor would care to profit by
A parent's power to make a child comply?
To win a lady's hand by such compulsion,
And not by love, would fill him with revulsion.
Don't, then, I beg you, urge my mother to make
Me bow to her authority for your sake.
Take back the love you offer, and reserve it
For some fine woman who will more deserve it.
TRISSOTIN.
Alas, what you command I cannot do.
I'm powerless to retract my love for you.
How shall I cease to worship you, unless
You cease to dazzle me with loveliness,
To stun my heart with beauty, to enthrall—
HENRIETTE.
Oh, come, Sir; no more nonsense. You have all
These Irises and Phyllises whose great
Attractiveness your verses celebrate,
And whom you so adore with so much art—

TRISSOTIN.
My mind speaks in those verses, not my heart.
I love those ladies in my poems merely,
While Henriette, alone, I love sincerely.
HENRIETTE.
Please, Sir—
TRISSOTIN.
     If by so speaking I offend,
I fear that my offense will never end.
My ardor, which I've hidden hitherto,
Belongs for all eternity to you;
I'll love you till this beating heart has stopped;
And, though you scorn the tactics I adopt,
I can't refuse your mother's aid in gaining
The joy I'm so desirous of obtaining.
If the sweet prize I long for can be won,
And you be mine, I care not how it's done.
HENRIETTE.
But don't you see that it's a risky course
To take possession of a heart by force;
That things, quite frankly, can go very ill
When a woman's made to wed against her will,
And that, in her resentment, she won't lack
For means to vex her spouse, and pay him back?
TRISSOTIN.
I've no anxiety about such things.
The wise man takes whatever fortune brings.
Transcending vulgar weaknesses, his mind
Looks down unmoved on mishaps of the kind,
Nor does he feel the least distress of soul
Regarding matters not in his control.
HENRIETTE.
You fascinate me, Sir; I'm much impressed.
I didn't know philosophy possessed
Such powers, and could teach men to endure
Such tricks of fate without discomfiture.
Your lofty patience ought, Sir, to be tested,
So that its greatness could be manifested;
It calls, Sir, for a wife who'd take delight
In making you display it, day and night;

But since I'm ill-equipped, by temperament,
To prove your virtue to its full extent,
I'll leave that joy to one more qualified,
And let some other woman be your bride.
TRISSOTIN.
Well, we shall see. The notary for whom
Your mother sent is in the neighboring room.

SCENE 2

Chrysale, Clitandre, Martine, Henriette

CHRYSALE.
Ah, daughter, I'm pleased indeed to find you here.
Prepare to show obedience now, my dear,
By doing as your father bids you do.
I'm going to teach your mother a thing or two;
And, first of all, as you can see, I mean
To thwart her will and reinstate Martine.
HENRIETTE.
I much admire the stands which you have taken.
Hold to them, Father; don't let yourself be shaken.
Be careful lest your kindly disposition
Induce you to abandon your position;
Cling to your resolutions, I entreat you,
And don't let Mother's stubbornness defeat you.
CHRYSALE.
What! So you take me for a booby, eh?
HENRIETTE.
Heavens, no!
CHRYSALE.
          Am I a milksop, would you say?
HENRIETTE.
I'd not say that.
CHRYSALE.
          Do you think I lack the sense
To stand up firmly for my sentiments?
HENRIETTE.
No, Father.

CHRYSALE.

                    Have I too little brain and spirit
To run my own house? If so, let me hear it.

HENRIETTE.

No, no.

CHRYSALE.

                 Am I the sort, do you suppose,
Who'd let a woman lead him by the nose?

HENRIETTE.

Of course not.

CHRYSALE.

                    Well then, what were you implying?
Your doubts of me were scarcely gratifying.

HENRIETTE.

I didn't mean to offend you, Heaven knows.

CHRYSALE.

Under this roof, my girl, what I say goes.

HENRIETTE.

True, Father.

CHRYSALE.

                No one but me has any right
To govern in this house.

HENRIETTE.

                        Yes, Father; quite.

CHRYSALE.

This is my family, and I'm sole head.

HENRIETTE.

That's so.

CHRYSALE.

              I'll name the man my child shall wed.

HENRIETTE.

Agreed!

CHRYSALE.

             By Heaven's laws, I rule your fate.

HENRIETTE.

Who questions that?

CHRYSALE.

                And I'll soon demonstrate
That, in your marriage, your mother has no voice,
And that you must accept your father's choice.

HENRIETTE.
Ah, Father, that's my dearest wish. I pray you,
Crown my desires by making me obey you.
CHRYSALE.
If my contentious wife should dare to take—
CLITANDRE.
She's coming, with the notary in her wake.
CHRYSALE.
Stand by me, all of you.
MARTINE.
                Trust me, Sir. I'm here
To back you up, if need be. Never fear.

SCENE 3

Philaminte, Bélise, Armande, Trissotin, the Notary, Chrysale,
Clitandre, Henriette, Martine

PHILAMINTE. (*To the Notary.*)
Can't you dispense with jargon, Sir, and write
Our contract in a style that's more polite?
THE NOTARY.
Our style is excellent, Madam; I'd be absurd
Were I to modify a single word.
PHILAMINTE.
Such barbarism, in the heart of France!
Can't you at least, for learning's sake, enhance
The document by putting the dowry down
In talent and drachma, rather than franc and crown?
And do use ides and calends for the date.
THE NOTARY.
If I did, Madam, what you advocate,
I should invite professional ostracism.
PHILAMINTE.
It's useless to contend with barbarism.
Come on, Sir; there's a writing-table here.
                (*Noticing Martine.*)
Ah! Impudent girl, how dare you reappear?
Why have you brought her back, Sir! Tell me why.

CHRYSALE.
I'll tell you that at leisure, by and by.
First, there's another matter to decide.
THE NOTARY.
Let us proceed with the contract. Where's the bride?
PHILAMINTE.
I'm giving away my younger daughter.
THE NOTARY.
                        I see.
CHRYSALE.
Yes. Henriette's her name, Sir. This is she.
THE NOTARY.
Good. And the bridegroom?
PHILAMINTE. (*Indicating Trissotin.*)
                      This is the man I choose.
CHRYSALE. (*Indicating Clitandre.*)
And I, for my part, have a bit of news:
This is the man she'll marry.
THE NOTARY.
                    Two grooms? The law
Regards that as excessive.
PHILAMINTE.
                  Don't hem and haw;
Just write down Trissotin, and your task is done.
CHRYSALE.
Write down Clitandre; he's to be my son.
THE NOTARY.
Kindly consult together, and agree
On a single person as the groom-to-be.
PHILAMINTE.
No, no, Sir, do as I have indicated.
CHRYSALE.
Come, come, put down the name which I have stated.
THE NOTARY.
First tell me by whose orders I should abide.
PHILAMINTE. (*To Chrysale.*)
What's this, Sir? Shall my wishes be defied?
CHRYSALE.
I won't stand by and let this fellow take
My daughter's hand just for my money's sake.

PHILAMINTE.
A lot your money matters to him! Indeed!
How dare you charge a learnèd man with greed?
CHRYSALE.
Clitandre shall marry her, as I said before.
PHILAMINTE. (*Pointing to Trissotin.*)
This is the man I've chosen. I'll hear no more.
The matter's settled, do you understand?
CHRYSALE.
My! For a woman, you have a heavy hand.
MARTINE.
It just ain't right for the wife to run the shop.
The man, I say, should always be on top.
CHRYSALE.
Well said.
MARTINE.
   Though I'm sacked ten times for saying so,
It's cocks, not hens, should be the ones to crow.
CHRYSALE.
Correct.
MARTINE.
   When a man's wife wears the breeches, folks
Snicker about him, and make nasty jokes.
CHRYSALE.
That's true.
MARTINE.
   If I had a husband, I wouldn't wish
For him to be all meek and womanish;
No, no, he'd be the captain of the ship,
And if I happened to give him any lip,
Or crossed him, he'd be right to slap my face
A time or two, to put me in my place.
CHRYSALE.
Sound thinking.
MARTINE.
   The master's heart is rightly set
On finding a proper man for Henriette.
CHRYSALE.
Yes.

MARTINE.
　　Well then, here's Clitandre. Why deny
The girl a fine young chap like him? And why
Give her a learnèd fool who prates and drones?
She needs a husband, not some bag of bones
Who'll teach her Greek, and be her Latin tutor.
This Trissotin, I tell you, just don't suit her.
CHRYSALE.
Right.
PHILAMINTE.
　　　　　We must let her chatter until she's through.
MARTINE.
Talk, talk, is all these pedants know how to do.
If I ever took a husband, I've always said,
It wouldn't be no learnèd man I'd wed.
Wit's not the thing you need around the house,
And it's no joy to have a bookish spouse.
When I get married, you can bet your life
My man will study nothing but his wife;
He'll have no other book to read but me,
And won't—so please you, Ma'am—know A from B.
PHILAMINTE.
Has your spokesman finished? And have I not politely
Listened to all her speeches?
CHRYSALE.
　　　　　　　　The girl spoke rightly.
PHILAMINTE.
Well then, to end all squabbling and delay,
Things now shall go exactly as I say.
　　　　　(Indicating Trissotin.)
Henriette shall wed this man at once, d'you hear?
Don't answer back; don't dare to interfere;
And if you've told Clitandre that he may wed
One of your daughters, give him Armande instead.
CHRYSALE.
Well! . . . There's one way to settle this argument.
　　　　　(To Henriette and Clitandre.)
What do you think of that? Will you consent?
HENRIETTE.
Oh, Father!

CLITANDRE.
> Oh, Sir!

BÉLISE.
> There's yet another bride
> By whom he might be yet more satisfied;
> But that can't be; the love we share is far
> Higher and purer than the morning star;
> Our bonds are solely of the intellect,
> And all extended substance we reject.

SCENE 4

Ariste, Chrysale, Philaminte, Bélise, Henriette, Armande,
Trissotin, the Notary, Clitandre, Martine

ARISTE.
> I hate to interrupt this happy affair
> By bringing you the tidings which I bear.
> You can't imagine what distress I feel
> At the shocking news these letters will reveal.
> > (*To Philaminte.*)
> This one's from your attorney.
> > (*To Chrysale.*)
> > And the other
> Is yours; it's from Lyons.

CHRYSALE.
> > What news, dear Brother,
> Could be so pressing, and distress you so?

ARISTE.
> There is your letter; read it, and you'll know.

PHILAMINTE. (*Reading.*)
> "Madam, I have asked your brother to convey to you this
> message, advising you of something which I dared not come and
> tell you in person. Owing to your great neglect of your affairs,
> the magistrate's clerk did not notify me of the preliminary
> hearing, and you have irrevocably lost your lawsuit, which you
> should in fact have won."

CHRYSALE. (*To Philaminte.*)
> You've lost your case!

PHILAMINTE.

My! Don't be shaken so!
I'm not disheartened by this trivial blow.
Do teach your heart to take a nobler stance
And brave, like me, the buffetings of chance.
"This negligence of yours has cost you forty thousand
crowns, for it is that amount, together with the legal
expenses, which the court has condemned you to pay."
Condemned! What shocking language! That's a word
Reserved for criminals.

ARISTE.

True; your lawyer erred,
And you're entirely right to be offended.
He should say that the court has *recommended*
That you comply with its decree, and pay
Forty thousand and costs without delay.

PHILAMINTE.

What's in this other letter?

CHRYSALE. (*Reading.*)

"Sir, my friendship with your brother leads me to take
an interest in all that concerns you. I know that you have
put your money in the hands of Argante and Damon, and I
regret to inform you that they have both, on the same day,
gone into bankruptcy."
Lost! All my money! Every penny of it!

PHILAMINTE.

What a shameful outburst, Sir. Come, rise above it!
The wise man doesn't mourn the loss of pelf;
His wealth lies not in things, but in himself.
Let's finish this affair, with no more fuss:

(*Pointing to Trissotin.*)

His fortune will suffice for all of us.

TRISSOTIN.

No, Madam, urge my cause no further. I see
That everyone's against this match and me,
And where I am not wanted, I shan't intrude.

PHILAMINTE.

Well! That's a sudden change of attitude.
It follows close on our misfortunes, Sir.

TRISSOTIN.
Weary of opposition, I prefer
To bow out gracefully, and to decline
A heart which will not freely yield to mine.
PHILAMINTE.
I see now what you are, Sir. I perceive
What, till this moment, I would not believe.
TRISSOTIN.
See what you like; I do not care one whit
What you perceive, or what you think of it.
I've too much self-respect to tolerate
The rude rebuffs I've suffered here of late:
Men of my worth should not be treated so:
Thus slighted, I shall make my bow, and go.
                              (*He leaves.*)
PHILAMINTE.
What a low-natured, mercenary beast!
He isn't philosophic in the least!
CLITANDRE.
Madam, I'm no philosopher; but still
I beg to share your fortunes, good or ill,
And dare to offer, together with my hand,
The little wealth I happen to command.
PHILAMINTE.
This generous gesture, Sir, I much admire,
And you deserve to have your heart's desire.
I grant your suit, Sir. Henriette and you—
HENRIETTE.
No, Mother, I've changed my mind. Forgive me, do,
If once more I oppose your plans for me.
CLITANDRE.
What! Will you cheat me of felicity,
Now that the rest have yielded, one and all?
HENRIETTE.
I know, Clitandre, that your wealth is small.
I wished to marry you so long as I
Might realize my sweetest hopes thereby,
And at the same time mend your circumstances.
But after this great blow to our finances,

I love you far too deeply to impose
On you the burden of our present woes.
CLITANDRE.
I welcome any fate which you will share,
And any fate, without you, I couldn't bear.
HENRIETTE.
So speaks the reckless heart of love; but let's
Be prudent, Sir, and thus avoid regrets.
Nothing so strains the bond of man and wife
As lacking the necessities of life,
And in the end, such dull and mean vexations
Can lead to quarrels and recriminations.
ARISTE. (*To Henriette.*)
Is there any reason, save the one you've cited,
Why you and Clitandre shouldn't be united?
HENRIETTE.
But for that cause, I never would say no;
I must refuse because I love him so.
ARISTE.
Then let the bells ring out for him and you.
The bad news which I brought was all untrue.
'T'was but a stratagem which I devised
In hopes to see your wishes realized
And undeceive my sister, showing her
The baseness of her pet philosopher.
CHRYSALE.
Now, Heaven be praised for that!
PHILAMINTE.

                       I'm overjoyed
To think how that false wretch will be annoyed,
And how the rich festivities of this
Glad marriage will torment his avarice.
CHRYSALE. (*To Clitandre.*)
Well, Son, our firmness has achieved success.
ARMANDE. (*To Philaminte.*)
Shall you sacrifice me to their happiness?
PHILAMINTE.
Daughter, your sacrifice will not be hard.
Philosophy will help you to regard
Their wedded joys with equanimity.

BÉLISE.
Let him be careful lest his love for me
Drive him, in desperation, to consent
To a rash marriage of which he will repent.
CHRYSALE. (*To the Notary.*)
Come, come, Sir, it is time your task was through;
Draw up the contract just as I told you to do.

PROPERTY LIST

On Stage—

Assorted drawing room furniture of the period
Books

Personal—

Verse (Trissotin)
2 letters (Ariste)
Note and books (Julien)

A NOTE FROM THE TRANSLATOR

This play is a study of the relation of learning to everyday life, and the cast is full of characters, both male and female, who display, in regard to learning, one or another kind of comic imbalance. The defects of the men are readily perceived: Chrysale, for example, is a philistine for whom a book is something in which to press his neckcloths; Trissotin and Vadius are vain and narrow pedants. The three "learned ladies," however, may be misunderstood unless they are seen unsentimentally and in their proper historical setting. Philaminte and her academy, as Act III makes plain, possess neither knowledge nor taste. Furthermore, it is not a hunger for self-improvement which motivates Philaminte, but a desire to seem distinguished, to "avenge" her sex, and to rise in society by means of holding a *salon*. This ill-motivated pseudo-intellectual woman has turned her sister-in-law Bélise into a fantast, and her daughter Armande into a neurotic poseur; she has also neglected or mismanaged the basic concerns of an upper-middle-class woman of her day: her household, her children, her business affairs. The healthiest attitudes toward the play's theme are embodied in, and expressed by, Clitandre and Henriette. The young lovers are witty, intelligent, tasteful, and independent-minded; they read books and form opinions of them; they do not, however, feel that the cultivation of the mind should estrange one from life's normal fulfillments and duties.

Clitandre's assertion that "A woman should know something . . . / Of every subject" was a very liberal sentiment for Molière's day. But Clitandre's liberalism, Henriette's attractively balanced nature, and the abnormality of the bluestockings will only be apparent to a modern audience if the play is so mounted as rather definitely to evoke its period. To "up-date" the set and costumes, in hopes of closely relating Molière's drama to contemporary feminism, would entail all sorts of misreading and anachronism. This has been sadly proven, I am told, by a recent modern-dress production of the original play in France.

The set should suggest the living-room of an upper-bourgeois house in seventeenth-century Paris. The general impression should be one of solidity and wealth. At the same time, the strange state of family affairs should be expressed by such means as shelves-full of books, busts of philosophers, astronomical instruments, charts, or a globe. Delivery of the lines should be letter-perfect, so as not to falsify the meter; yet within the artifice of the verse the actors should try to speak as naturally as possible. The characters' names should be pronounced in a manner *approximately* French, but without strain.

R. W.

NEW PLAYS

★ **THE CREDEAUX CANVAS by Keith Bunin.** A forged painting leads to tragedy among friends. "There is that moment between adolescence and middle age when being disaffected looks attractive. Witness the enduring appeal of Prince Hamlet, Jake Barnes and James Dean, on the stage, page and screen. Or, more immediately, take a look at the lithe young things in THE CREDEAUX CANVAS..." *–NY Times.* "THE CREDEAUX CANVAS is the third recent play about painters...it turned out to be the best of the lot, better even than most plays about non-painters." *–NY Magazine.* [2M, 2W] ISBN: 0-8222-1838-0

★ **THE DIARY OF ANNE FRANK by Frances Goodrich and Albert Hackett, newly adapted by Wendy Kesselman.** A transcendently powerful new adaptation in which Anne Frank emerges from history a living, lyrical, intensely gifted young girl. "Undeniably moving. It shatters the heart. The evening never lets us forget the inhuman darkness waiting to claim its incandescently human heroine." *–NY Times.* "A sensitive, stirring and thoroughly engaging new adaptation." *–NY Newsday.* "A powerful new version that moves the audience to gasps, then tears." *–A.P.* "One of the year's ten best." *– Time Magazine.* [5M, 5W, 3 extras] ISBN: 0-8222-1718-X

★ **THE BOOK OF LIZ by David Sedaris and Amy Sedaris.** Sister Elizabeth Donderstock makes the cheese balls that support her religious community, but feeling unappreciated among the Squeamish, she decides to try her luck in the outside world. "...[a] delightfully off-key, off-color hymn to clichés we all live by, whether we know it or not." *–NY Times.* "Good-natured, goofy and frequently hilarious..." *–NY Newsday.* "...[THE BOOK OF LIZ] may well be the world's first Amish picaresque...hilarious..." *–Village Voice.* [2M, 2W (doubling, flexible casting to 8M, 7W)] ISBN: 0-8222-1827-5

★ **JAR THE FLOOR by Cheryl L. West.** A quartet of black women spanning four generations makes up this hilarious and heartwarming dramatic comedy. "...a moving and hilarious account of a black family sparring in a Chicago suburb..." *–NY Magazine.* "...heart-to-heart confrontations and surprising revelations...first-rate..." *–NY Daily News.* "...unpretentious good feelings...bubble through West's loving and humorous play..." *–Star-Ledger.* "...one of the wisest plays I've seen in ages...[from] a master playwright." *–USA Today.* [5W] ISBN: 0-8222-1809-7

★ **THIEF RIVER by Lee Blessing.** Love between two men over decades is explored in this incisive portrait of coming to terms with who you are. "Mr. Blessing unspools the plot ingeniously, skipping back and forth in time as the details require...an absorbing evening." *–NY Times.* "...wistful and sweet-spirited..." *–Variety.* [6M] ISBN: 0-8222-1839-9

★ **THE BEGINNING OF AUGUST by Tom Donaghy.** When Jackie's wife abruptly and mysteriously leaves him and their infant daughter, a pungently comic reevaluation of suburban life ensues. "Donaghy holds a cracked mirror up to the contemporary American family, anatomizing its frailties and miscommunications in fractured language that can be both funny and poignant." *–The Philadelphia Inquirer.* "...[A] sharp, eccentric new comedy. Pungently funny...fresh and precise..." *–LA Times.* [3M, 2W] ISBN: 0-8222-1786-4

★ **OUTSTANDING MEN'S MONOLOGUES 2001–2002 and OUTSTANDING WOMEN'S MONOLOGUES 2001–2002 edited by Craig Pospisil.** Drawn exclusively from Dramatists Play Service publications, these collections for actors feature over fifty monologues each and include an enormous range of voices, subject matter and characters. MEN'S ISBN: 0-8222-1821-6 WOMEN'S ISBN: 0-8222-1822-4

DRAMATISTS PLAY SERVICE, INC.
440 Park Avenue South, New York, NY 10016 212-683-8960 Fax 212-213-1539
postmaster@dramatists.com www.dramatists.com

NEW PLAYS

★ **A LESSON BEFORE DYING by Romulus Linney, based on the novel by Ernest J. Gaines.** An innocent young man is condemned to death in backwoods Louisiana and must learn to die with dignity. "The story's wrenching power lies not in its outrage but in the almost inexplicable grace the characters must muster as their only resistance to being treated like lesser beings." –*The New Yorker*. "Irresistable momentum and a cathartic explosion...a powerful inevitability." –*NY Times*. [5M, 2W] ISBN: 0-8222-1785-6

★ **BOOM TOWN by Jeff Daniels.** A searing drama mixing small-town love, politics and the consequences of betrayal. "...a brutally honest, contemporary foray into classic themes, exploring what moves people to lie, cheat, love and dream. By BOOM TOWN's climactic end there are no secrets, only bare truth." –*Oakland Press*. "...some of the most electrifying writing Daniels has ever done..." –*Ann Arbor News*. [2M, 1W] ISBN: 0-8222-1760-0

★ **INCORRUPTIBLE by Michael Hollinger.** When a motley order of medieval monks learns their patron saint no longer works miracles, a larcenous, one-eyed minstrel shows them an outrageous new way to pay old debts. "A lightning-fast farce, rich in both verbal and physical humor." –*American Theatre*. "Everything fits snugly in this funny, endearing black comedy...an artful blend of the mock-formal and the anachronistically breezy...A piece of remarkably dexterous craftsmanship." –*Philadelphia Inquirer*. "A farcical romp, scintillating and irreverent." –*Philadelphia Weekly*. [5M, 3W] ISBN: 0-8222-1787-2

★ **CELLINI by John Patrick Shanley.** Chronicles the life of the original "Renaissance Man," Benvenuto Cellini, the sixteenth-century Italian sculptor and man-about-town. Adapted from the autobiography of Benvenuto Cellini, translated by J. Addington Symonds. "[Shanley] has created a convincing Cellini, not neglecting his dark side, and a trim, vigorous, fast-moving show." –*BackStage*. "Very entertaining...With sharp purpose, the narrative undermines chronology before untangling it...touching and funny..." –*NY Times*. [7M, 2W (doubling)] ISBN: 0-8222-1808-9

★ **PRAYING FOR RAIN by Robert Vaughan.** Examines a burst of fatal violence and its aftermath in a suburban high school. "Thought provoking and compelling." –*Denver Post*. "Vaughan's powerful drama offers hope and possibilities." –*Theatre.com*. "[The play] doesn't put forth compact, tidy answers to the problem of youth violence. What it does offer is a compelling exploration of the forces that influence an individual's choices, and of the proverbial lifelines—be they familial, communal, religious or political—that tragically slacken when society gives in to apathy, fear and self-doubt..." –*Westword*."...a symphony of anger..." –*Gazette Telegraph*. [4M, 3W] ISBN: 0-8222-1807-0

★ **GOD'S MAN IN TEXAS by David Rambo.** When a young pastor takes over one of the most prestigious Baptist churches from a rip-roaring old preacher-entrepreneur, all hell breaks loose. "...the pick of the litter of all the works at the Humana Festival..." –*Providence Journal*. "...a wealth of both drama and comedy in the struggle for power..." –*LA Times*. "...the first act is so funny...deepens in the second act into a sobering portrait of fear, hope and self-delusion..." –*Columbus Dispatch*. [3M] ISBN: 0-8222-1801-1

★ **JESUS HOPPED THE 'A' TRAIN by Stephen Adly Guirgis.** A probing, intense portrait of lives behind bars at Rikers Island. "...fire-breathing...whenever it appears that JESUS is settling into familiar territory, it slides right beneath expectations into another, fresher direction. It has the courage of its intellectual restlessness...[JESUS HOPPED THE 'A' TRAIN] has been written in flame." –*NY Times*. [4M, 1W] ISBN: 0-8222-1799-6

DRAMATISTS PLAY SERVICE, INC.
440 Park Avenue South, New York, NY 10016 212-683-8960 Fax 212-213-1539
postmaster@dramatists.com www.dramatists.com

NEW PLAYS

★ **THE CIDER HOUSE RULES, PARTS 1 & 2 by Peter Parnell, adapted from the novel by John Irving.** Spanning eight decades of American life, this adaptation from the Irving novel tells the story of Dr. Wilbur Larch, founder of the St. Cloud's, Maine orphanage and hospital, and of the complex father-son relationship he develops with the young orphan Homer Wells. "...luxurious digressions, confident pacing...an enterprise of scope and vigor..." *–NY Times.* "...The fact that I can't wait to see Part 2 only begins to suggest just how good it is..." *–NY Daily News.* "...engrossing...an odyssey that has only one major shortcoming: It comes to an end." *–Seattle Times.* "...outstanding...captures the humor, the humility...of Irving's 588-page novel..." *–Seattle Post-Intelligencer.* [9M, 10W, doubling, flexible casting] PART 1 ISBN: 0-8222-1725-2 PART 2 ISBN: 0-8222-1726-0

★ **TEN UNKNOWNS by Jon Robin Baitz.** An iconoclastic American painter in his seventies has his life turned upside down by an art dealer and his ex-boyfriend. "...breadth and complexity...a sweet and delicate harmony rises from the four cast members...Mr. Baitz is without peer among his contemporaries in creating dialogue that spontaneously conveys a character's social context and moral limitations..." *–NY Times.* "...darkly funny, brilliantly desperate comedy...TEN UNKNOWNS vibrates with vital voices." *–NY Post.* [3M, 1W] ISBN: 0-8222-1826-7

★ **BOOK OF DAYS by Lanford Wilson.** A small-town actress playing St. Joan struggles to expose a murder. "...[Wilson's] best work since *Fifth of July*...An intriguing, prismatic and thoroughly engrossing depiction of contemporary small-town life with a murder mystery at its core...a splendid evening of theater..." *–Variety.* "...fascinating...a densely populated, unpredictable little world." *–St. Louis Post-Dispatch.* [6M, 5W] ISBN: 0-8222-1767-8

★ **THE SYRINGA TREE by Pamela Gien.** Winner of the 2001 Obie Award. A breathtakingly beautiful tale of growing up white in apartheid South Africa. "Instantly engaging, exotic, complex, deeply shocking...a thoroughly persuasive transport to a time and a place...stun[s] with the power of a gut punch..." *–NY Times.* "Astonishing...affecting ...[with] a dramatic and heartbreaking conclusion...A deceptive sweet simplicity haunts THE SYRINGA TREE..." *–A.P.* [1W (or flexible cast)] ISBN: 0-8222-1792-9

★ **COYOTE ON A FENCE by Bruce Graham.** An emotionally riveting look at capital punishment. "The language is as precise as it is profane, provoking both troubling thought and the occasional cheerful laugh...will change you a little before it lets go of you." *–Cincinnati CityBeat.* "...excellent theater in every way..." *–Philadelphia City Paper.* [3M, 1W] ISBN: 0-8222-1738-4

★ **THE PLAY ABOUT THE BABY by Edward Albee.** Concerns a young couple who have just had a baby and the strange turn of events that transpire when they are visited by an older man and woman. "An invaluable self-portrait of sorts from one of the few genuinely great living American dramatists...rockets into that special corner of theater heaven where words shoot off like fireworks into dazzling patterns and hues." *–NY Times.* "An exhilarating, wicked...emotional terrorism." *–NY Newsday.* [2M, 2W] ISBN: 0-8222-1814-3

★ **FORCE CONTINUUM by Kia Corthron.** Tensions among black and white police officers and the neighborhoods they serve form the backdrop of this discomfiting look at life in the inner city. "The creator of this intense...new play is a singular voice among American playwrights...exceptionally eloquent..." *–NY Times.* "...a rich subject and a wise attitude." *–NY Post.* [6M, 2W, 1 boy] ISBN: 0-8222-1817-8

DRAMATISTS PLAY SERVICE, INC.
440 Park Avenue South, New York, NY 10016 212-683-8960 Fax 212-213-1539
postmaster@dramatists.com www.dramatists.com